Judgment by Code

Judgment by Code

When Artificial Intelligence Takes the Bench

Corin Hale

Mindful Pages

Published in 2025

ISBN: 9789371774697 (PB)
ISBN: 9789371770538 (eBook)

Published by

Mindful Pages
Imprint of Alpha Editions LLC
312 W. 2nd St #1834
Casper, WY 82601, USA

This book was developed using advanced writing tools to support the drafting and ideation process. All content has been thoughtfully curated, refined, and reviewed to ensure quality and relevance.

Content

Introduction
When Machines Meet Judgment

In courtrooms around the globe, judgment has long been the province of human minds—individuals schooled not merely in statutes and precedent, but in discernment, empathy, and the nuanced rhythms of the communities they serve. That familiar picture is beginning to fracture. Algorithms now suggest sentencing ranges, evaluate bail, draft contracts, and advise clients, all with a speed and economy unattainable by human practitioners. Tasks once synonymous with professional judgement are increasingly treated as problems of data, optimisation, and computational efficiency.

This shift is more than technological—it is cultural and conceptual. AI in law does not merely assist; it subtly reshapes the meaning of legal reasoning itself. The central claim of *Judgment by Code* is that this is a watershed moment, one that demands a sober reckoning with the boundaries of automation and the nature of human judgement.

Law has always been more than rules and procedures. It is a social contract, embedded in history, moral complexity, and shared values. Interpretation has mattered as much as codification. Algorithms, for all their sophistication, do not interpret—they process. They do not reason—they optimise. They do not deliberate—they calculate probabilities. When such systems are tasked with mediating disputes, assessing fairness, or influencing determinations of guilt, what is lost in translation? Efficiency may rise, but deliberation, context, and nuance risk being sacrificed.

At the heart of the book's argument is a simple, yet profound premise: legal systems are fundamentally human. Their imperfections, ambiguities, and allowances for dissent are not flaws—they are essential features, enabling justice to accommodate the complexities of lived experience. AI, by contrast, operates on closure and predictability. It excels at pattern recognition and probabilistic modelling, but it cannot apprehend the full range of human intention, ethical variance, or emotional subtlety. When algorithms take the bench, the letter of the law may endure, but the spirit of judgment is irrevocably altered.

Consider the growing presence of AI across legal infrastructure. Courts employ algorithmic tools to streamline caseloads; governments use predictive models to screen asylum applications or detect welfare fraud; corporations deploy contract analysis software capable of performing in seconds tasks that once required teams of lawyers. Efficiency and standardisation are real gains, yet the pressing question is ethical: what form of justice are we encoding into these systems?

The stakes are far from abstract. Risk assessment tools in the United States, like COMPAS, claim to predict reoffending objectively, yet investigations reveal embedded racial biases and opaque scoring mechanisms, disproportionately impacting marginalised communities. Predictive policing software relies on historical data shaped by decades of discriminatory enforcement. These systems inherit both the efficiencies and inequities of the societies that produce them. Far from neutral, they are mirrors of existing social hierarchies.

Opacity compounds the problem. Proprietary algorithms, complex machine-learning processes, and trade secrets make many AI tools effectively black boxes. Yet the law demands transparency, accountability, and explainability. This tension—between algorithmic inscrutability and the requirements of legitimate legal authority—represents one of the most pressing crises in contemporary justice.

Judgment by Code does not advocate a wholesale rejection of AI. Rather, it calls for discernment. The question is not whether AI can perform legal tasks, but whether it should. Automating parking fines is not equivalent to delegating child custody rulings to software. Drafting template contracts differs fundamentally from offering legal counsel. Recognising these distinctions—and the ethical stakes each entails—is essential.

The book interrogates the philosophical and moral foundations of legal reasoning, asking readers to confront difficult questions: what constitutes judgment? Can moral discretion ever be codified? Should all aspects of legal procedure be automated merely because technology allows it? And if not, where—and by whom—is the boundary drawn?

The text unfolds across eleven chapters, beginning with a contrast between the interpretive fluidity of common law and the procedural rigidity of algorithms. Judges often embrace ambiguity as an invitation to reason; algorithms see it as a problem to be resolved, sometimes prematurely. This tension—between human adaptability and computational certainty—recurs throughout.

Subsequent chapters examine the crisis of authority that emerges when decision-making shifts from bench to code. AI increasingly wields real power, often with limited oversight, appeal, or moral accountability. Who bears responsibility when the system errs? Can we trust decisions that cannot be explained in human terms?

The book then confronts law's uncodifiable core: its moral, emotional, and contextual dimensions. Discretion, empathy, and nuanced judgement are not bugs—they are safeguards of justice. Programming them into code, if possible, risks distortion or oversimplification. Later sections explore AI's encroachment into the practice of law itself, from chatbots drafting arguments to compliance tools advising corporations, raising questions of legitimacy, professional identity, and responsibility.

Scale and efficiency, while alluring, carry trade-offs. Can algorithmic mass processing preserve fairness, due process, and individuality? Often, the answer is uncertain. Bias too remains a persistent challenge: historical data embeds prejudice; design decisions carry the blind spots of creators. Addressing these issues requires more than better datasets—it demands a systemic engagement with the values we choose to automate.

The book culminates with questions of expertise and governance. What remains the domain of human legal professionals in an era when machines outperform humans in technical tasks? How do we preserve the uniquely human capacity for judgment? How can regulation, consent, and oversight ensure that AI serves justice rather than undermines it? Finally, it addresses what should never be delegated to machines: family law rulings, asylum determinations, and judgements that require moral discernment. These are not appeals to nostalgia, but acknowledgements of the limits of computation in moral and social life.

Judgment by Code offers neither simple solutions nor technological prescriptions. It provides a framework for thinking critically about the intersection of law and artificial intelligence, intended for legal professionals, policymakers, technologists, and citizens who understand that justice is too vital to be entrusted to automation alone. It equips readers to ask incisive questions, delineate ethical boundaries, and participate in shaping a legal future that is not only efficient, but fundamentally just.

Let us begin.

Chapter 1
Code vs. Common Law

The law has always been a creature of language—messy, evolving, and weighted with meaning. Its force lies not only in what it dictates, but in how it is read, by whom, and under what circumstances. A statute is never merely a rule; it is an invitation to interpretation, a point of departure in an ongoing dialogue between text, precedent, institutional norms, and lived experience. Legal reasoning, therefore, resembles navigating a complex argument rather than solving a tidy equation—it relies as much on analogy, principle, and ethical judgement as on logical parsing. Herein lies the first tension between traditional law and artificial intelligence: law tolerates ambiguity; code abhors it.

When AI enters the legal sphere, it brings a fundamentally different conception of "understanding." Algorithms detect patterns, apply probabilistic models, and produce outputs optimised for predictive accuracy or efficiency. They compute; they do not deliberate. Their strength is scale, speed, and statistical coherence—not ethical nuance or moral sensitivity. Yet it is precisely within these grey zones—hard cases, conflicting interests, morally fraught contexts—that law derives legitimacy and earns trust. This chapter begins by establishing a framework for comparing humanistic legal interpretation with computational methodologies, revealing not merely a difference in technique, but a profound divergence in epistemology and values.

Common law systems prize precedent, not as determinism, but as dialogue. A ruling carries the momentum of past decisions while shaping the possibilities of future judgments. Dissenting opinions often gain significance over time, signalling shifts in societal norms and interpretive priorities. Cases are not isolated; they exist on a continuum, embedded in historical, cultural, and moral contexts. Legal reasoning is recursive, interpretive, and inherently contextual.

AI systems, by contrast, flatten this complexity. When trained to identify relevant legal information or predict case outcomes, machines treat prior decisions as static data points. They do not absorb the tension of moral ambiguity, public sentiment, or dissenting voices that may later become law. They cannot grasp the weight of a survivor's testimony or the normative resonance of a judge's careful phrasing. Patterns substitute for principles, creating the illusion that legal reasoning is reducible to computation and that justice is measurable like a ledger.

Take contract analysis tools, for instance. AI now sifts through vast numbers of agreements to flag risk clauses, propose amendments, or benchmark terms. For routine matters, these systems are indispensable: they save hours, reduce error, and standardise language. Yet they also reinforce a mechanistic conception of law—as compliance rather than as relational strategy. In complex negotiations, contract clauses reflect trust, leverage, and context; what the algorithm flags as anomalous may be precisely the bespoke term that embodies the spirit of the agreement.

Automated compliance systems reveal a similar tension. Regulators and corporations increasingly rely on AI to flag violations, inconsistencies, or regulatory risk. These tools operate on fixed thresholds, triggering alerts when parameters are breached. But compliance is rarely that simple. Intent, proportionality, and context matter. Was a breach deliberate or incidental? Does it signal systemic failure or a one-off error? Machines rarely ask these questions; humans do. Reducing compliance to binary outcomes risks turning oversight into a procedural ritual that captures surface irregularities while missing structural problems.

This epistemological gap underscores a fundamental divide between legal judgment and algorithmic reasoning. Legal interpretation thrives on ambiguity because ambiguity is generative. Multiple plausible readings allow law to evolve, absorb new values, and remain responsive to society. Courts reconcile competing interests, weigh intentions, and sometimes defy precedent when justice demands it. Machines, by contrast, optimise for consistency, selecting the statistically probable outcome rather than the ethically defensible one. Ambiguity is a problem for code; for the jurist, it is opportunity.

The implications are tangible. Judicial sentencing tools trained on prior cases promise efficiency, neutrality, and consistency. Yet they inherit historical biases and often lack transparency in how risk scores are calculated. Defendants may face harsher sentences because an opaque algorithm deems them high-risk, with no way for courts—or the public—to scrutinise the underlying data. Here, the challenge is jurisprudential, not merely technical: we delegate human consequences to systems devoid of moral and interpretive capacity.

Machines can apply legal rules—they already do, and often with precision—but judgment is a different matter. It demands knowing when to apply a rule, when to interpret broadly or narrowly, when to challenge precedent, and when exceptions are warranted. It requires contextual sensitivity, ethical awareness, and engagement with the human consequences of decisions. No algorithm, however sophisticated, possesses these faculties.

Human judgment is imperfect, biased, and fallible. Yet it is accountable. Decisions can be challenged, debated, and appealed. They exist within a moral and institutional framework acknowledging error. Machines lack this kind of accountability. Their authority flows from performance metrics or corporate assurances, not deliberative legitimacy or social consent.

Moreover, AI design often resists the contestation that law demands. Courts must reason and justify rulings; many AI outputs are inscrutable, derived from complex models that cannot be interrogated or reversed. This asymmetry threatens due process: when humans are judged by systems they cannot understand or contest, foundational principles of justice erode.

The notion of value-neutral AI is a myth. Every system embodies assumptions—about fairness, risk, relevance, or harm—that are technical in form but deeply political in effect. A recidivism-predicting model may disproportionately penalise marginalised communities; a contract analysis tool may prioritise corporate efficiency at the expense of equitable outcomes. Machine logic is not neutral—it is ideology made executable.

We are witnessing not merely automation of tasks, but the encroachment of a mode of reasoning privileging correlation over causation, consistency over deliberation, and prediction over principle. Scale, speed, and statistical insight are strengths—but if left unchecked, they risk hollowing out law's normative core.

This chapter invites readers to grapple with that tension. It traces the philosophy of legal interpretation, the epistemology of machine reasoning, and the points of collision between the two. The critical question is whether the legal system we build will reflect our collective aspirations for justice—or simply mirror the efficiencies of code.

We begin not with technical manuals, but with an inquiry into rules, meaning, and judgment. Entrusting machines with legal authority demands that we first confront what it truly means to judge—not merely to process inputs, but to understand, deliberate, and decide. The stakes are nothing less than the integrity of justice itself.

The Architecture of Interpretation

A law is never just a rule. It is a gesture toward meaning, a distillation of social values, historical memory, and normative intention encoded in language. Unlike code, which demands precision and tolerates no ambiguity, legal language thrives precisely because it can absorb multiple meanings. This elasticity is not a flaw but a deliberate feature. It is what allows legal systems to adapt to new circumstances, to account for moral nuance, and to serve justice not merely as mechanical application, but as human judgment exercised in context. The architecture of legal interpretation, then, is not built on deterministic logic—it is scaffolded by uncertainty, argumentation, and the living fabric of society itself.

This is why the introduction of artificial intelligence into legal reasoning introduces such friction. AI systems, no matter how advanced, are engineered for clarity, closure, and optimisation. They parse language not for layered meaning but for extractable signals; they do not interpret, they infer. When such systems are tasked with processing legal information, they do so according to a radically different architecture of logic—one that prioritises computational tractability over hermeneutic depth. The result is a growing epistemic gap between the normative aspirations of law and the probabilistic output of machines.

To appreciate this divergence, consider how courts and judges approach ambiguity. In legal interpretation, ambiguity is not an obstacle to be avoided; it is a starting point for deliberation. A single word in a statute—*reasonable*, *necessary*, *good faith*—can provoke extensive judicial debate and multiple layers of analysis. Judges will consult legislative history, consider competing canons of construction, draw analogies to prior cases, and weigh the broader consequences of one reading over another. They may even diverge in their interpretations, with majority and dissenting opinions shaping the legal landscape in tandem. This interpretive pluralism is not a failure of the system—it is its strength. It allows the law to evolve organically, to incorporate dissent, and to remain responsive to the values of the community it serves.

Contrast this with how AI systems handle ambiguity. Natural language processing models trained on legal texts treat words as tokens mapped to numerical vectors in multidimensional space. Meaning is derived statistically, based on co-occurrence and context patterns within the training data. Ambiguity, in this paradigm, is something to be resolved automatically, often by selecting the most probable interpretation based on frequency or proximity. This probabilistic approach may work well for tasks like document classification or legal summarisation, but it strips language of its interpretive richness. It assumes that the "right" meaning is the one most often used in similar contexts, rather than the one most appropriate to a unique case. In doing so, it collapses the interpretive space into a set of statistical likelihoods, severed from the deliberative process that gives law its legitimacy.

This problem is not merely technical—it is conceptual. Legal reasoning, particularly in common law traditions, is structured by a complex interplay between text and context, between rules and their exceptions. The same statute may be applied differently across jurisdictions, times, and circumstances, because its application is shaped by a web of historical precedents, institutional norms, and societal expectations. Legal meaning is not a fixed property of the text, but a product of its performance in situated acts of reasoning. In this sense, interpretation is not something that follows the rule—it *is* the rule, constantly remade in the act of application.

AI, however, operates on a different ontology. It treats rules as fixed entities and seeks to generalise their application across datasets. The logic is reductive: take past inputs and outcomes, identify patterns, and predict future decisions. This works best when the task is well-bounded, the rules are explicit, and the data is clean. But law resists these conditions by design. Consider the legal concept of *mens rea*, or guilty mind. Determining intent in a criminal case often requires an intricate reconstruction of events, motivations, and subjective states. It involves reading between the lines of testimony, interpreting silences, and weighing the credibility of witnesses. No machine learning model, no matter how refined, can access the interiority that this demands. It can only approximate it through proxies—words used, actions taken, statistical correlations. But proxies are not judgments. They are shadows cast by the real thing.

Even in more structured domains of law, such as tax or administrative regulation, the limits of AI's interpretive capacity quickly become evident. Take a regulation that requires a business to make "reasonable efforts" to comply with a reporting requirement. What constitutes "reasonable" may depend on industry norms, resource constraints, evolving technologies, or prior case law. A judge might evaluate these factors holistically, considering the spirit of the law and the conduct's broader context. An AI system, by contrast, would likely treat "reasonable efforts" as a pattern-matching exercise, inferring what has been considered reasonable in the past without engaging in principled reasoning about what *ought* to be deemed reasonable now. The result may be a decision that is statistically defensible, but normatively hollow.

This distinction becomes even sharper when we consider the role of dissent in legal systems. Dissenting opinions, often sidelined in computational models, are essential to legal evolution. They preserve minority views, introduce new interpretive frameworks, and sometimes become the majority position in future cases. Their presence signals that law is not just a set of rules, but a field of contestation where values, reasoning styles, and worldviews collide. AI systems trained to prioritise consensus or majoritarian outcomes inherently devalue dissent. In doing so, they risk reinforcing dominant perspectives while marginalising those that challenge the status quo—often the very perspectives that drive progress in legal thought.

There is also a profound temporal tension between the logic of code and the logic of law. AI systems learn from the past to predict the future. Their strength lies in extrapolating from historical data to identify likely outcomes. But legal interpretation often involves a forward-looking dimension—judges may rule in ways that set new standards, anticipate future harms, or reshape social expectations. They are not merely interpreters of what *has been*, but architects of what *ought to be*. In this way, legal reasoning is as much about norm creation as it is about norm application. Machines can simulate the former, but they cannot originate it. They lack the normative imagination required to extend the law into new domains or reframe existing doctrines in light of changing ethical landscapes.

To appreciate the implications of this difference, consider the challenge of regulating emerging technologies such as facial recognition or gene editing. In these domains, precedents are scarce, and legal texts may be silent or outdated. Interpreting the law requires analogical reasoning, moral deliberation, and public engagement. It demands that legal actors not only apply existing norms, but interrogate their relevance and scope. This is the opposite of what machine learning models do. They perform best in high-data, low-novelty environments—where the future resembles the past and ambiguity is minimal. When faced with radically new contexts, their performance degrades or becomes erratic. Legal systems, by contrast, are built to evolve in the face of novelty. They thrive on interpretation precisely because it allows the law to meet the future on its own terms.

One might argue that these limitations are temporary—that with better data, more sophisticated models, and improved natural language understanding, AI will eventually master legal interpretation. But this view misunderstands the nature of interpretation itself. It is not merely a problem of complexity to be solved; it is a mode of human reasoning that integrates affect, ethics, social awareness, and reflective judgment. Interpretation involves caring about outcomes, taking responsibility for decisions, and engaging in public justification. These are not technical attributes—they are moral and civic ones. Until machines can share in those responsibilities, they will remain tools, not interpreters.

This is not to say that AI has no place in legal reasoning. On the contrary, when designed thoughtfully and deployed with care, it can enhance legal analysis, uncover patterns of bias, and assist with information retrieval on a scale impossible for humans. But we must be clear about what it can and cannot do. It can process language, but it does not *understand* it. It can predict outcomes, but it does not *reason* toward them. It can replicate decisions, but it does not *justify* them. These distinctions matter—not only because they clarify the boundaries of AI's utility, but because they protect the core of what makes legal judgment legitimate in the first place.

Legal systems are not merely systems of rules. They are systems of meaning, of memory, of moral struggle. Their architecture is interpretive because human life is interpretive. It is shaped by history, context, conflict, and conscience. The law's authority comes not from its infallibility, but from its capacity to engage these forces openly, reflectively, and with accountability. If we are to preserve that authority in the age of intelligent machines, we must ensure that the architecture of interpretation remains intact—and remains human.

Law as a Living System

There is a persistent misconception that the law is static—etched into statute books, immune to interpretation, and immune from change. In truth, it is a dynamic system, continuously shaped by human reasoning, social currents, and institutional dialogue. Unlike software code, which is designed for clarity, predictability, and rigid execution, the law thrives on argument, dissent, and the evolution of meaning over time. To treat law as a system of fixed instructions is to fundamentally misunderstand its nature. *Law is not simply enforced—it is lived, interpreted, and constantly remado.* This is not a matter of philosophical abstraction; it is an operational reality of every functioning legal system, especially in jurisdictions shaped by common law traditions. Yet it is precisely this living character of the law that artificial intelligence, as currently designed, is least equipped to model, let alone respect.

The vitality of law is most evident in its case-based development. In common law systems, legal authority accumulates incrementally, through the resolution of specific disputes. Courts do not legislate in the formal sense, but their judgments carry precedential weight. This creates a jurisprudential lineage: each case builds on prior ones, distinguishing, refining, or occasionally overturning them. The result is not a uniform rulebook, but a layered structure of decisions—some consonant, others conflicting—bound together by legal reasoning rather than by mere textual command. The strength of this system lies in its responsiveness. A court facing a novel case does not merely retrieve a pre-written rule; it engages in an act of interpretation, balancing the force of precedent against the demands of present justice.

Dissenting opinions, often sidelined in discussions of legal authority, are a crucial mechanism in this process. They preserve alternate reasoning paths and serve as reservoirs of future doctrine. What appears today as a minority view may, through social and judicial shifts, become tomorrow's orthodoxy. Consider the trajectory of American civil rights jurisprudence. Justice Harlan's dissent in *Plessy v. Ferguson* (1896), in which he wrote that "our Constitution is colour-blind," was once a minority view. Decades later, that sentiment underpinned *Brown v. Board of Education* (1954), which overturned the doctrine of "separate but equal." A machine trained solely on historical majorities would miss the long arc of moral and legal progression. *What dissent preserves is the unfinishedness of law—the idea that what is lawful is not always what is just, and that today's outlier may be tomorrow's compass.*

Legal reasoning also adapts in response to cultural change. Courts are not sealed chambers of logic; they are embedded in societies that evolve. Issues such as gender identity, environmental protection, and digital privacy demonstrate how rapidly legal understandings can shift. For instance, the interpretation of what constitutes "cruel and unusual punishment" under the Eighth Amendment in the United

States has changed dramatically over time, reflecting changing societal standards. A machine trained on past rulings might reproduce obsolete views, mistaking legal inertia for authority. But human judges, attentive to context and guided by conscience, can reframe old principles for new circumstances. This is what gives the law its durability—it remains anchored in tradition while being capable of moral growth.

AI systems trained on historical legal data do not operate in this evolutionary mode. They extract patterns, assign probabilities, and generate outputs based on observed regularities. This is not interpretation in the legal sense; it is statistical projection. The algorithm does not know why a precedent was set, why it was later narrowed, or what normative debates surrounded its application. It treats legal change as an anomaly to be flattened rather than a signal to be understood. Its logic assumes that the past is the best guide to the future—an assumption that collapses in moments of legal or social transformation. When Roe v. Wade was overturned in *Dobbs v. Jackson Women's Health Organization* (2022), it was not because the prior rule had lost predictive accuracy. It was because the ideological composition of the court had changed and with it, the interpretive frame through which constitutional principles were understood. *Such shifts cannot be modelled by counting case frequencies—they require interpretive agency, historical awareness, and moral reasoning.*

This flattening effect is particularly dangerous in legal systems where marginalised communities have historically lacked visibility. AI systems trained on legal corpora reflect the decisions that were documented, prioritised, and preserved. What they often miss are the voices that were excluded—cases never brought, harms never recognised, arguments dismissed out of hand. Predictive models built on these datasets can perpetuate the status quo under the guise of objectivity. This is not a neutral oversight—it is a re-inscription of structural inequity through statistical inference. A system that predicts based on what *has been* without asking *why* those outcomes occurred is not merely conservative; it is complicit.

Legal systems, at their best, are designed to contest this inertia. The principle of stare decisis—respect for precedent—is balanced by doctrines that permit its departure. Courts may distinguish, limit, or overrule prior decisions when fidelity to justice demands it. This flexibility is not algorithmic; it is deliberative. It requires judges to consider not only the factual matrix of the case but also the evolving standards of decency, fairness, and reasonableness within the society they serve. Such standards are not fixed inputs—they are contested, emergent, and irreducibly human.

There is a fundamental asymmetry, then, between the way law changes and the way AI systems learn. Machine learning models, especially those built on supervised learning, improve by being exposed to more of the same. Their performance is optimised when the test data resembles the training data. They do not seek to question their parameters—they are calibrated to reinforce them. Legal reasoning, by contrast, improves by being exposed to what is different. It matures by confronting hard cases, moral dilemmas, and interpretive conflict. *The vitality of law lies not in how often it replicates itself, but in how it adapts to challenges that strain its assumptions.*

This does not mean that legal reasoning is chaotic or arbitrary. The best judges reason through principles, analogies, and structured deliberation. But they do so with an awareness that rules are tools, not ends. The goal is not consistency for its own sake, but justice attuned to circumstance. Machines, however, struggle to weigh circumstance unless it is already coded as a variable. They cannot intuit significance from silence or infer context from cultural change. Their understanding is inductive, not reflective. They see what happened, not what might have happened had the world been more just.

The limits of formalisation are nowhere more apparent than in areas like family law, refugee adjudication, or indigenous rights—domains where the particulars matter profoundly. A decision about custody is not just about legal eligibility; it is about the welfare of a child, the integrity of kinship, the emotional stability of households. Such cases require an ability to hear what is not said, to interpret narrative gaps, and to balance legal criteria with human compassion. These are not attributes of systems trained on formal rule application. They are the domain of empathy-infused judgment, which emerges from experience, deliberation, and ethical attunement.

Even in commercial law, which might appear more amenable to automation, the law's living quality asserts itself. Contract disputes, for example, often hinge on what the parties *intended*, not merely on what they *wrote*. Courts will examine conduct, negotiations, and surrounding circumstances. A contract clause that appears clear in isolation may be ambiguous in context. This is why interpretation cannot be reduced to text mining or clause-matching. It is a relational act, shaped by culture, expectation, and legal history.

When legal reasoning is viewed as a living system, the inadequacy of machine formalisation becomes clearer. Formal systems aim to reduce variation, eliminate ambiguity, and lock meaning into reproducible outputs. Living systems, by contrast, accommodate ambiguity as a means of resilience. They change because people change—because values shift, because societies reckon with their failures, and because new generations see justice differently. To model law as a closed system of rules is not only to misrepresent its nature—it is to preclude its evolution.

This is not an argument against the use of AI in law, but for humility in its application. Machine systems can assist with legal research, document review, and even standardised decision support. But they should not be mistaken for participants in legal reasoning. They do not dissent, reflect, or reform. They do not remember differently, hope radically, or mourn injustices yet unredressed. Only human systems—constrained though they are—have the moral and institutional infrastructure to do that. And it is only by preserving the law's status as a living system that we can ensure it remains fit to serve the society it claims to represent.

What Machines Do With Rules

The most compelling illusion surrounding artificial intelligence in law is that machines "understand" rules. They do not. What they do is *simulate* understanding by recognising patterns, parsing syntax, and generating outputs that resemble legal reasoning. This distinction is more than semantic. It defines the boundary between computational efficiency and normative judgment. Where a lawyer applies a rule in context, often reshaping its meaning to accommodate ambiguity, competing values, or evolving norms, AI systems encode rules in ways that treat interpretation as a statistical artefact, not a deliberative act. The result is a surface-level mimicry that can be dazzling in speed and scale, but shallow in legal depth and blind to the moral architecture in which rules are embedded.

Artificial intelligence processes rules not as statements of intent or invitations to reasoning, but as data points that correlate with prior outcomes. In machine learning applications—especially those based on supervised learning—models are fed thousands or millions of labelled examples. In the legal domain, these examples might be judicial opinions, annotated contracts, regulatory filings, or case summaries. The goal is not to uncover meaning but to detect statistical regularities: that certain clauses frequently lead to certain risks; that certain words or patterns are associated with certain decisions. The machine doesn't *know* that "force majeure" clauses deal with unforeseen catastrophes. It identifies the term as a cluster of characters that tend to appear near discussions of disruption, liability, or insurance. The semblance of legal knowledge is built entirely on co-occurrence and frequency, not comprehension or context.

This approach can yield powerful results in domains where legal language is highly regularised. Contract review software, for instance, has been widely adopted in corporate law firms and in-house legal departments. Tools like Kira Systems, Luminance, or LawGeex can process thousands of agreements in minutes, flagging clauses that deviate from standard practice, suggesting language improvements, or identifying obligations across document portfolios. These systems are not mere keyword scanners—they use sophisticated NLP techniques to "read" documents and tag relevant provisions. But crucially, their evaluation is statistical, not normative. They determine that a clause is risky because it is *unusual*, not because it fails a substantive ethical or strategic test. They can spot a missing indemnity clause but cannot assess whether the clause present is *fair*, *negotiated in good faith*, or *appropriate for the parties involved.* That judgment still belongs to a human.

The same structural limitation appears in AI systems designed for regulatory compliance. Tools like Ascent or Ayasdi aim to automate the interpretation of complex regulatory frameworks, helping banks and corporations track obligations across jurisdictions and identify gaps in their practices. These platforms can rapidly ingest changes to regulation, match them against corporate policies, and generate alerts when discrepancies arise. What they cannot do is make discretionary judgments about proportionality, intent, or legal nuance. A financial regulation that instructs institutions to maintain "adequate" capital buffers or implement "reasonable" risk controls invites a debate about standards, not just thresholds. A compliance officer or regulator might weigh market volatility, business models, or evolving supervisory expectations. AI tools, unless explicitly configured to include such considerations, treat these terms as triggers for binary classification. *The interpretive judgment that turns a legal rule into a fair, enforceable norm remains outside the machine's grasp.*

This is not a failure of engineering. It is a consequence of design priorities. Machine learning systems are optimised for tasks where high-volume data and measurable outcomes are available. Legal reasoning often resists these conditions. In court decisions, the same statute may be applied in contradictory ways across cases. Judges write opinions that blend logic, precedent, moral reasoning, and rhetorical persuasion. Their decisions often hinge not on black-letter rules, but on exceptions, analogies, and equities. A case may be decided *against* the statistical majority of prior rulings precisely because a new fact pattern demands fresh reasoning. From a computational standpoint, such "exceptions" look like noise or outliers. From a legal standpoint, they are the system doing its job.

The divergence is particularly stark in predictive justice tools. Software used to forecast litigation outcomes, sentencing ranges, or bail decisions—such as COMPAS in the U.S. or HART in the U.K.—relies on historical data to generate risk scores. These tools are marketed as objective aids to human decision-makers, but their outputs often rest on opaque assumptions and unexamined proxies. A risk score derived from past arrest data may reproduce patterns of racial profiling or economic disadvantage, even if race or income is not explicitly included as a feature. The model doesn't "intend" to discriminate; it simply optimises for past outcomes. *Yet if the past is unjust, prediction becomes a vehicle for injustice disguised as efficiency.*

The problem is not merely that machines "don't get" the law. It's that they get it in ways that distort its moral content. In automating legal analysis, AI systems risk reducing the law to a set of statistical regularities, drained of the principled disagreement and deliberative flexibility that give it meaning. A contract, in this paradigm, becomes a set of clause frequencies; a regulation becomes a checklist; a judgment becomes a vector of features mapped to a binary label. This mode of reasoning can be useful—it accelerates routine analysis and can surface patterns invisible to the human eye. But it must not be mistaken for legal reasoning itself.

There is also a danger of performance overshadowing understanding. When AI tools deliver outputs that appear legally coherent, users may defer to them without scrutiny. This is especially true in high-volume or low-stakes contexts, where efficiency pressures dominate. Legal professionals, under tight deadlines or constrained budgets, may lean heavily on AI tools to flag risks or suggest strategies. But deference to these outputs assumes that the model's logic is aligned with the user's objectives—an assumption that often goes untested. *The veneer of precision can mask a void of interpretation.* If the tool flags a clause as "non-standard," what does that mean in a specific negotiation? Non-standard for whom? In what jurisdiction? With what consequence? These are questions machines cannot answer meaningfully on their own.

To be clear, some attempts have been made to inject normative parameters into legal AI. Rule-based systems—unlike data-driven models—can encode logic trees or regulatory taxonomies that reflect human judgments about compliance. Hybrid approaches try to combine statistical modelling with expert-curated features or legal ontologies. These methods improve transparency and allow for some degree of auditability. But they also expose the trade-off at the heart of legal AI: the more interpretive subtlety you try to encode, the less scalable and generalisable the system becomes. Law, unlike code, often resists formalisation beyond a certain point. It bends toward context, not abstraction.

Consider the difference between a traffic fine and a refugee asylum claim. The former is highly rule-bound: if you drove 15 km/h over the limit, you are fined. The latter demands deep human interpretation: was the applicant's fear of persecution well-founded? Is their testimony credible? Are country conditions consistent with their account? No matter how much data is available, the evaluative core of such decisions cannot be meaningfully outsourced. Machines can assist—by highlighting inconsistencies or retrieving precedents—but they cannot *weigh* lives, balance rights, or imagine alternative futures. That remains a human task.

In the context of emerging legal fields—digital rights, climate accountability, bioethics—the gap between prediction and judgment only widens. These areas often lack precedent, involve novel harms, and depend on forward-looking interpretations. Legal professionals must frame arguments in terms of principles and policy impacts, not just text and precedent. AI systems, unless radically reimagined, have little to offer in these zones of moral creativity. *What they do with rules is replicate; what law often requires is invention.*

None of this is to say that AI should be kept out of legal work. Its contributions can be significant when matched to the right tasks: document classification, due diligence, discovery, compliance monitoring. But the seductive belief that machines can "understand" and apply the law autonomously must be resisted. The law is not merely a system of rules; it is a system of judgment. It requires interpretation, disagreement, and moral vision. Until AI systems can argue in bad faith, admit doubt, or stand accountable for harm, they remain processors of rules—not participants in the practice of law. Recognising this is not a constraint on innovation; it is a safeguard for justice.

The Gap Between Rule and Judgment

A machine can tell you that a contract clause appears 37 percent more often in high-risk agreements. It can predict that a defendant is statistically more likely to reoffend based on demographic and behavioural indicators. It can flag a line in a regulatory filing as anomalous when benchmarked against comparable submissions. What it cannot do—what no algorithm has yet convincingly demonstrated—is exercise *judgment.* This distinction is neither semantic nor peripheral; it strikes at the heart of the legal enterprise. Law is not a field of pure rule application. It is a field of *judgment under conditions of uncertainty*, where the answer often depends not on what the rule is, but on what it *ought* to mean in a specific context.

Judgment is the faculty that allows us to see when a rule should be stretched or tempered, when precedent ought to be distinguished, and when exceptions are not merely justified but necessary. It is what enables a judge to weigh competing principles, reconcile factual ambiguities, and recognise when formal equality produces substantive injustice. In many cases, the law is clear on paper but contested in application. AI systems, however, treat clarity as a precondition for functionality. Their operational logic assumes that rules are stable, that inputs are consistent, and that the task is to find the statistically optimal mapping from one to the other. Yet legal systems are built, in part, to accommodate conflict, exception, and evolution—not just compliance.

The implications are evident in the realm of sentencing. Risk assessment tools like COMPAS in the United States or HART in the United Kingdom are designed to support bail and parole decisions. These systems use prior case data to forecast the likelihood of reoffending, often relying on variables like age, employment history, and previous convictions. But the leap from *risk* to *recommendation* is where the conceptual fracture occurs. The algorithm does not—and cannot—account for redemption, remorse, systemic bias in policing, or the broader social costs of incarceration. It outputs a score; the human judge must interpret it. And yet, the score is often treated as if it *is* judgment—an evidentiary object with the sheen of objectivity, even when its underlying logic is hidden behind proprietary code.

This substitution of prediction for judgment has consequences far beyond the courtroom. In immigration adjudication, for instance, automated triage tools are being explored to streamline case processing. The aim is efficiency: identify likely approvals or denials early, fast-track routine cases, and reduce backlog. But refugee claims often hinge on the credibility of personal narratives, the interpretation of country conditions, or the psychological impact of trauma—features that do not reduce cleanly into structured data fields. A claim that looks statistically weak may be legally and morally compelling. An AI tool trained on historical outcomes may simply learn to mimic the biases and blind spots of the past. *When a machine learns what we have done, it does not ask whether we should have done it.*

The conceptual flaw here is subtle but dangerous: the assumption that legal decision-making is a matter of pattern recognition, rather than moral reasoning. This assumption is encouraged by the superficial similarity between legal doctrine and computational rules. Both involve formal systems, procedural steps, and conditional logic. But similarity in structure does not imply equivalence in function. A legal rule must be interpreted in light of its purpose, its context, and its consequences. The exercise of judgment involves reasoning with analogies, navigating ambiguity, and accepting that no algorithm can fully resolve normative disagreement. Two judges may read the same statute, apply the same precedent, and still reach different conclusions—each plausible, each justified by different principles or perspectives. *This is not a failure of the system; it is an expression of its depth.*

The rule of law, as understood in liberal democratic systems, depends on this depth. It is not merely that rules are followed, but that those who apply them are accountable, reflective, and capable of justifying their decisions in terms intelligible to the public. Legal systems do not function merely by applying rules to facts—they function by *arguing about what the rules mean*, *how the facts are constructed*, and *what justice requires*. AI, by contrast, provides outputs, not arguments. It does not reason in the public sphere. It does not participate in a tradition of legal discourse. It cannot dissent, revise, or reflect. It can approximate outcomes, but it cannot *explain why a different outcome might also be valid.*

This is especially critical when law intersects with emerging technologies or evolving social norms. Consider cases involving online speech, data privacy, or reproductive rights. The legal framework may be underdetermined, the precedents conflicted, and the societal values in flux. A judge facing such a case must exercise interpretive creativity, draw on broader moral frameworks, and anticipate the ripple effects of their ruling. An AI system trained on past outcomes is, by definition, backward-looking. It cannot intuit new principles, propose doctrinal shifts, or imagine jurisprudential futures. It offers a simulation of past decisions, not a deliberation about future ones.

Some have argued that with sufficient data and sufficiently advanced models, AI will eventually learn to simulate judgment so well that the distinction becomes moot. But this argument misunderstands the nature of judgment itself. It is not just about output accuracy; it is about *ownership*, *accountability*, and *normative responsibility*. When a judge hands down a controversial ruling, they are required to explain it, defend it, and accept public scrutiny. They can be challenged, reversed, or overruled. Their authority rests not on predictive reliability but on their institutional role, their reasoning, and their responsiveness to the values of the community. AI systems, however, are often deployed without these mechanisms. Their creators may be unknown, their reasoning opaque, and their accountability diffused. *To substitute such systems for judgment is to displace not just human discretion but democratic legitimacy.*

Moreover, legal judgment often involves *refusing* to apply a rule. A judge may nullify a law for being unconstitutional, decline enforcement on the grounds of proportionality, or invoke equity to achieve a fairer outcome. These are not acts of error or inconsistency—they are expressions of the law's capacity to correct itself from within. An AI system, bound to its training data and optimisation goals, has no such capacity. It cannot ask whether the rule itself is flawed, whether the structure of authority should be challenged, or whether justice lies in *not* deciding according to precedent. *The power to withhold judgment—or to subvert the logic of rule-following in service of higher principles—is what defines the moral weight of legal responsibility.*

In areas of law that demand deep ethical sensitivity—child protection, end-of-life decisions, transitional justice—the absence of true judgment is not merely a technical limitation; it is a moral abdication. It is one thing to assist with document review or litigation forecasting. It is another to place life-altering decisions in the hands of systems that cannot feel, reflect, or understand suffering. AI systems can process the fact that someone is a minor, has a disability, or comes from a war zone. But they do not comprehend vulnerability, injustice, or hope. They cannot imagine what it means to be the subject of the law, to live under its authority, or to appeal to it as a source of protection.

This is not an argument for preserving human judgment because it is always superior in outcome. Humans, too, are fallible, biased, and inconsistent. But the failings of human judgment occur within a structure of ethical responsibility and institutional redress. When a judge errs, the system has tools for correction—appeals, reviews, public accountability. When an algorithm errs, we often do not even recognise the error until it has scaled harm across hundreds or thousands of decisions. And even then, identifying responsibility becomes a game of attribution—designer, deployer, user, regulator—with no clear lines of answerability.

The central dilemma, then, is not whether AI can apply rules. It clearly can—and in many domains, it does so efficiently. The dilemma is whether we want legal systems to be governed by rule-application alone, or whether we insist that judgment must remain at the core of law. That question cannot be resolved by reference to accuracy rates or throughput metrics. It requires a deeper reflection on what law is for, what kind of community it serves, and what kind of authority we are willing to accept. In the age of machine decision-making, the gap between rule and judgment is not a design flaw to be closed. It is a moral space to be protected. Only within that space can justice, in any meaningful sense, continue to live.

Chapter 2
The Authority Crisis

A judge's ruling has always carried more than the weight of law; it bears the unmistakable imprint of human responsibility. For all its formalism, the courtroom has traditionally functioned as a theatre of accountability—public, contestable, and narratively traceable. Even when we disagree with outcomes, we know who issued them, the reasoning invoked, and the avenues for appeal. The deliberate rhythms of justice—debate, dissent, principled reasoning—are not inefficiencies but structural safeguards that confer legitimacy. When decision-making moves from the bench to an algorithm, from a named individual to an opaque model, the nature of authority itself changes. Law becomes codified as computation, yet it becomes strangely unmoored. Who is responsible? By what logic? On what grounds may decisions be challenged? Increasingly, the answers are obscured by layers of code, corporate secrecy, and automated abstraction.

This is the crisis of authority: a severing of power from accountability, a shift in the locus of responsibility. It arises not merely because AI participates in legal processes, but because it does so without clear integration into the moral and institutional frameworks that underpin justice. A judge who errs can be appealed; a legislature that missteps can be voted out. But an algorithm deployed by a contractor, trained on private datasets, calibrated by unknown engineers, and acquired with minimal public oversight—who answers when it harms? In theory, these systems are instruments; in practice, they function as discretionary actors, shaping lives through parole recommendations, sentencing guidelines, credit assessments, and asylum triage. Yet they neither deliberate nor explain. They calculate.

Nowhere is this more evident than in the criminal justice system. Across the United States, risk-assessment tools such as COMPAS or PSA are used to estimate a defendant's likelihood of reoffending or failing to appear in court. These systems assign numerical scores based on age, criminal history, employment, and other factors, guiding judicial decisions on bail or release. Efficiency, consistency, and objectivity are the stated aims. But when a person's liberty hinges on a score generated by a proprietary algorithm—one hidden from both defendant and counsel—the courtroom transforms into a black box. The rule of law presumes transparency, contestability, and reason-giving. Algorithmic authority delivers none of these. It instructs without explaining, predicts without justifying, and adjudicates without accountability.

Opacity is not a technological inevitability—it is frequently a design choice. Leading legal-tech tools are developed by private companies asserting intellectual property rights over their models, data, and scoring processes. While legally defensible, this stance directly conflicts with the public's right to transparency in justice. If the state relies on a model to curtail liberty, that model should be open to scrutiny. Yet courts have repeatedly upheld vendor secrecy over defendants' rights. The paradox is striking: in striving to make justice more efficient through automation, we simultaneously render it less knowable, less contestable, and less legitimate.

Similar concerns arise in finance. Lenders increasingly deploy machine-learning models to evaluate creditworthiness, drawing on vast datasets including transaction histories and behavioural patterns. These models evolve continuously, often beyond the capacity of even the institutions themselves to fully audit. Applicants denied loans receive vague explanations—"insufficient credit history," "high-risk profile"—with no clarity on which factors mattered or how to challenge the outcome. Decision-making becomes centralised, opaque, and inscrutable. Governance, once rooted in rules and reasoning, is displaced by scoring systems whose internal logic is intentionally hidden.

The erosion of accountability compounds the problem. Traditional legal institutions operate on the principle that power must be exercised within frameworks of justification and appeal: judges write opinions, legislators face elections, police officers answer to complaints. AI systems, by contrast, often bypass these rituals. They are deployed without public consultation, refined without ethical oversight, and when failures occur, they are treated as technical glitches rather than moral failings. A judge who misapplies the law may face review; an algorithm that perpetuates injustice across thousands of cases is deemed a coding problem. Metrics replace moral responsibility, and the expectation that decision-makers answer to those affected diminishes.

Even when safeguards exist, they are ill-equipped for distributed algorithmic authority. A bail recommendation may be shaped by proprietary software, enacted through local court policies, influenced by state procurement, and informed by external data agencies. Responsibility fragments; accountability diffuses. Contesting such decisions becomes arduous, systemic correction nearly impossible. Public trust erodes. When the holders of authority are invisible, and when recourse is opaque, the legitimacy of the legal system itself is jeopardised.

Perhaps the most insidious feature of this crisis is the illusion of neutrality. AI is often presented as objective, fair, and consistent, masking the fact that every system reflects its creators' assumptions and values. Choices about data selection, outcome labelling, variable weighting, and definitions of risk or fairness are inherently political. Once embedded in software, these decisions are obscured behind interfaces that appear impartial. Treating machine outputs as authoritative transfers these unexamined assumptions into practice, stripping away spaces for debate, scrutiny, and ethical reflection.

Human judgment carries moral weight: it is process as well as product, a form of engagement with competing arguments, lived experience, and normative reasoning. Judges listen, deliberate, and justify their decisions; they can be questioned, challenged, and appealed. AI systems exist outside this moral infrastructure. They cannot testify, respond to cross-examination, or evolve through principled debate. Their "judgments" emerge from optimisation goals, not ethical reflection. To equate such outputs with legal authority is misleading and corrosive to justice itself.

The central question becomes pressing: whose judgment counts? When AI shapes legal outcomes, whose values define fairness, harm, and risk? Who interrogates these assumptions, and by what mechanism? These are not peripheral concerns; they touch the core of democratic governance and institutional legitimacy. A system that affects rights without accountability is not merely flawed—it is unjust.

This authority crisis is thus not simply about automation. It is about hollowing out law's normative core through the delegation of judgment to opaque systems. It is about the rise of invisible power, operating beyond scrutiny, presented as unassailable. It marks a shift from deliberative institutions to predictive infrastructures, whose authority derives not from public consent but from proprietary logic and bureaucratic convenience.

This chapter traces that shift in detail, examining how algorithms have become de facto decision-makers across legal and quasi-legal domains—from criminal justice and immigration to financial regulation and child welfare. It interrogates the myth of neutrality surrounding these systems and exposes the design choices that embed opacity at their core. Above all, it presses the central question: what must remain human in the practice of justice? If judgment is one such element, then no matter how powerful our technologies become, they must remain subordinate to institutions that are transparent, contestable, and morally accountable to the public they serve.

From Human Bench to Algorithmic Black Box

A courtroom is more than a place where rules are applied; it is a forum where human reasoning, responsibility, and morality are made visible. Every judgement rendered by a judge is a performance of authority—anchored in legal reasoning, tempered by discretion, and ultimately accountable to the public. The very visibility of the human bench—its procedures, language, and rituals—is part of what gives it legitimacy. When decision-making is transferred from this open deliberative space to algorithmic systems that few understand and none can interrogate meaningfully, something critical is lost. The law becomes not only automated but *obscured*, detached from the mechanisms of democratic oversight and institutional transparency that define justice in practice. We move from courts of record to systems of inference, from reasoning in public to calculating in private.

This transition is already well underway in systems that quietly shape liberty, creditworthiness, and access to opportunity. In jurisdictions across the United States and beyond, courts increasingly rely on risk assessment algorithms to inform bail and parole decisions. These tools, such as COMPAS (Correctional Offender Management Profiling for Alternative Sanctions) or the Public Safety Assessment (PSA), produce numeric scores meant to predict the likelihood that a defendant will fail to appear for trial or commit a future offence. Judges are encouraged—sometimes even required—to consider these scores in determining whether a person should be released pretrial. On the surface, these tools promise greater consistency and reduced reliance on subjective judgment. In practice, they introduce a new form of opacity. The scores are the product of proprietary models trained on historical data that may reflect past patterns of discrimination, institutional bias, or flawed record-keeping. A defendant may learn they have been denied bail based on a "high risk" designation, but they cannot see the factors behind the score or challenge the model's logic. Defence attorneys may be left arguing against an invisible adversary—one that offers no rationale and accepts no cross-examination.

Proponents of algorithmic decision-making in bail and parole contexts often point to empirical gains: reductions in jail populations, streamlined case processing, and improved accuracy in predicting certain outcomes. Yet these metrics conceal the deeper trade-offs being made. Accuracy in prediction does not equate to fairness in judgment. A model may correctly identify that younger defendants with prior misdemeanours have a higher statistical likelihood of reoffending—but such correlations do not justify treating every individual within that group as if they were the same. The risk score flattens the particulars of the case into a generalised output. It offers no room for narrative, no space for personal context, and no recognition of change. It predicts what is most likely, not what is just.

The same structural issues surface in credit scoring, where algorithmic models determine access to mortgages, personal loans, and consumer financing. Tools like FICO and VantageScore—alongside newer fintech models trained on behavioural data—evaluate individuals' creditworthiness using a mix of financial history, purchasing behaviour, and, in some cases, alternative data such as mobile usage patterns or geolocation. These systems operate largely without transparency. Consumers denied credit are offered vague explanations: "too many recent inquiries" or "credit utilisation too high." The deeper logic of the decision—the weight assigned to each variable, the interaction between factors, the presence of potential proxies for race or income—is inaccessible. Regulators struggle to audit these models, not only because the algorithms are proprietary, but because many are designed to be non-interpretable by default. In pursuit of performance, they are optimised for predictive power, not human understanding.

The shift from human to algorithmic decision-making is not merely a change in tools; it is a reconfiguration of power. Human judges, for all their imperfections, are embedded in institutions designed to support contestation, appeal, and public reasoning. They are trained to justify their rulings, exposed to scrutiny by media and civil society, and held to standards of consistency, transparency, and fairness. Algorithmic systems, by contrast, operate without such institutional moorings. They are developed by private firms, tuned by data scientists, implemented by administrators, and shielded by intellectual property law. Their decisions—if they can be called that—are the result of probabilistic calculations, not interpretive reasoning. They lack not only empathy but explainability, not only discretion but visibility. *The courtroom, once a space of argument and accountability, risks becoming a site of silent automation—where outcomes are dictated by systems whose rationale no one can see or contest.*

This shift raises urgent questions about legitimacy. If a person is denied bail, rejected for credit, or flagged for further investigation based on an algorithmic score, to whom can they appeal? The judge may defer to the score. The developer may claim trade secret protections. The administrator may point to procurement decisions. The chain of accountability collapses. Unlike in traditional legal decisions, where the author of the judgment is identifiable and the reasoning is open to critique, algorithmic systems disperse responsibility across technical, bureaucratic, and commercial domains. No one actor can explain the decision in full, nor is anyone clearly liable for its harms.

Some defenders of these systems argue that they simply support—not supplant—human judgment. Judges remain free to overrule algorithmic recommendations, lenders can override credit scores, and parole boards retain ultimate discretion. But in practice, deference to machine outputs is common, especially when those outputs are framed as objective or data-driven. Over time, the human role shifts from *judging* to *rubber-stamping*. The algorithm becomes the silent authority in the room, its logic rarely challenged, its recommendations quietly followed. The very language of decision-making changes: judges speak of "the tool's assessment," banks refer to "the model's output," and policymakers defer to "what the data shows." In this environment, discretion is hollowed out and accountability dispersed. *The system continues to operate, but its centre of gravity has moved—from visible actors to invisible infrastructures.*

What emerges is a new kind of legal actor: the algorithmic agent whose authority is implicit, unaccountable, and unpersoned. It is not a judge, not a lawyer, not a clerk, but it shapes outcomes with profound legal and moral consequences. It exists without subjectivity or explanation. It does not reason with principle, does not respond to contestation, does not evolve through public dialogue. Yet it acts. And because it acts within institutions that carry the force of law, its presence raises foundational questions: What does it mean for the law to be applied by a system that cannot explain itself? What becomes of justice when decisions are justified only by statistical likelihood? Who do we become when we treat automated outputs as self-legitimating?

There are those who see this transition as inevitable—a technological evolution of institutional decision-making. But inevitability is not a defence. The introduction of algorithmic systems into legal domains requires active choices about what we value: speed or deliberation, consistency or flexibility, efficiency or empathy. It forces us to decide whether we will accept opacity in the name of performance, and whether we will tolerate decisions without accountability if they come wrapped in data. These are not technical questions; they are constitutional ones. They speak to the kind of society we wish to be, and to the standards we set for institutions that govern our lives.

The move from the human bench to the algorithmic black box is not simply a story about innovation. It is a reckoning with authority, responsibility, and the role of reason in public life. The bench, for all its flaws, was at least *visible*. It spoke in words, reasoned in public, and could be questioned. The black box does none of these. It calculates, scores, outputs—and disappears. If we are to preserve the moral and democratic integrity of our legal systems, we must insist that those who exercise power, whether human or machine-assisted, do so in ways that are intelligible, contestable, and accountable. Anything less is not judgment—it is administration without justice.

Legitimacy Without Accountability

A system does not gain legitimacy merely by functioning. It earns it through a structure of authority that is visible, contestable, and grounded in public justification. In legal and political institutions, legitimacy depends on a reciprocal relationship between decision-makers and the people affected by their decisions. Laws are drafted through legislative processes, adjudicated by named judges, and enforced by officers of the state—all within frameworks that allow for critique, appeal, and change. But when AI systems are deployed to make decisions that shape lives—granting loans, predicting recidivism, approving visas, flagging fraud—they often bypass the mechanisms that generate legitimacy. These systems *wield real power*, but they are not elected, appointed, sworn in, or publicly accountable. They operate in shadow, not as a side effect of complexity, but because opacity is embedded in their very architecture.

Trust in legal authority is not automatic; it is built through transparency, responsiveness, and the capacity to give reasons. Yet AI systems increasingly influence outcomes in courts, public services, and financial institutions without offering any of those things. A parole applicant denied release based on a "risk score" may have no access to the data or reasoning behind that score. A welfare recipient flagged by an algorithm for suspected fraud might never see the evidence used to trigger the investigation. Even if the decisions are formally reviewed by human actors, the default presumption often favours the system's recommendation—precisely because it appears data-driven and objective. But *objectivity without explanation is not neutrality—it is unaccountable power dressed in statistical credibility.*

The problem deepens when such systems are protected from scrutiny by commercial interests. Many of the tools used in high-stakes legal and quasi-legal contexts are developed by private vendors who assert intellectual property rights over their models and data pipelines. Governments, courts, and agencies that rely on these tools are often contractually barred from inspecting their inner workings. This creates an extraordinary asymmetry: an individual can be affected—sometimes irrevocably—by a decision whose logic is not only opaque but deliberately shielded from public view. When challenged, officials often respond not with principled defence, but with deferral: "The system flagged it," or "The algorithm made the recommendation." In these moments, *authority flows not from deliberation, but from code—and no one takes responsibility for the outcome.*

The erosion of accountability is not limited to public institutions. In the financial sector, machine learning models determine who qualifies for a mortgage, what interest rates they are offered, and how their creditworthiness is assessed. The logic behind these models is often inscrutable even to the institutions that deploy them. Engineers train models on vast data sets, optimise them for accuracy or risk reduction, and ship them into production. But the decision boundaries formed by these systems are emergent properties—not explicitly coded, but inferred from patterns in the data. The result is that a person may be denied a loan because of their online browsing habits, their zip code, or the linguistic features of their application, with no clear explanation as to why. *Even when required by law to provide a justification, companies often respond with generic outputs—boilerplate statements that conceal more than they reveal.*

What is at stake here is more than procedural fairness. It is the question of what qualifies a system to make decisions in the first place. In democratic societies, decision-making authority is meant to be authorised by the public, constrained by law, and subject to redress. AI systems, by contrast, are often introduced without public debate, evaluated on narrow performance metrics, and shielded from appeal by their technical opacity. They enter the legal and administrative ecosystem not through democratic mandate but through procurement—acquired like office furniture or payroll software. Their legitimacy is assumed rather than earned, conferred by institutions eager to modernise, streamline, or "innovate" under budgetary constraints. *This shift marks a departure from the principle that power should be visible, traceable, and morally justified.*

The danger is compounded by a widespread belief in the neutrality of computation. Because algorithms are framed as technical artefacts—designed to optimise, not to judge—they are granted a presumption of fairness that human decision-makers no longer enjoy. But every AI system reflects human choices: what data to include, which objectives to optimise, how to weigh trade-offs, and what counts as error. These choices are not value-free; they are deeply political. A predictive policing model trained on historical arrest data will reproduce the biases embedded in past enforcement. A credit scoring algorithm optimised for default risk may disproportionately penalise the poor, the young, or the undocumented. These outcomes are not "biases" in the narrow statistical sense; they are the material consequences of design decisions made without public input, ethical deliberation, or regulatory oversight.

The response from developers and institutions is often to invoke technical fixes: de-bias the data, add fairness constraints, build explainability layers. These efforts are important, but insufficient. *No technical solution can substitute for the political work of accountability.* A system that produces "fair" outcomes by one statistical metric may still fail to respect the dignity, agency, and legal rights of those it affects. A system that is technically interpretable may still be too complex for meaningful public scrutiny. The problem is not simply that algorithms are flawed—it is that they are deployed in ways that systematically evade the structures of legitimacy that govern other forms of public authority.

Attempts to regulate these systems have so far struggled to catch up. Existing legal frameworks—whether rooted in data protection, administrative law, or anti-discrimination statutes—were not designed for algorithmic environments. They assume identifiable actors, traceable decision chains, and interpretable justifications. AI systems blur these lines. Responsibility is distributed across designers, operators, regulators, and users. The decision itself is not always clearly demarcated. Was it the training data that produced the outcome? The model architecture? The input variables? The threshold settings? Accountability fragments under the weight of technical complexity. *In place of rule-based governance, we are left with an ecosystem of informal norms, implicit assumptions, and invisible delegations of power.*

This transformation undermines not only individual rights, but public trust. When people feel that decisions affecting their freedom, finances, or status are made by systems they cannot see, understand, or challenge, their confidence in the institutions that deploy those systems begins to erode. The legitimacy crisis becomes social as well as institutional. It breeds cynicism, detachment, and resistance—not only to technology, but to the broader project of democratic governance. Rebuilding trust requires more than better interfaces or clearer disclaimers. It requires a return to first principles: *Who gets to decide? On what grounds? And to whom are they accountable?*

Some technologists argue that the answer lies in better design—building ethical AI, aligning machine learning with human values, or developing governance-by-architecture. These are valuable aspirations, but they risk substituting design solutions for political ones. Legitimacy cannot be engineered; it must be earned through processes that are participatory, deliberative, and revisable. That means embedding AI systems in institutional structures that reflect public values, permit contestation, and accept correction. It means treating AI not as a neutral tool, but as a legal and moral actor—one that must be held to the same standards of transparency, justification, and responsibility as any other authority that exercises public power.

The real challenge is not that AI systems are making decisions. It is that they are doing so without the ethical, legal, and institutional scaffolding that makes decision-making legitimate. *Power without accountability is not authority—it is risk disguised as progress.* If we are to preserve the moral foundations of law and governance in the age of algorithmic decision-making, we must insist that every exercise of power—human or machine-assisted—be answerable to the people it affects. Anything less is not innovation. It is abdication.

Opacity as Design, Not Flaw

One of the most persistent misconceptions surrounding algorithmic systems in law is that opacity is a technical limitation—an unfortunate side effect of model complexity or the inherent difficulty of machine learning explainability. In reality, opacity in many legal-tech systems is not accidental; it is intentional. It is engineered, safeguarded, and contractually reinforced to protect commercial interests, shield operational assumptions from scrutiny, and pre-empt uncomfortable debates about embedded bias. In a legal system where transparency is not only a value but a precondition for legitimacy, the proliferation of deliberately inscrutable decision-making tools marks a fundamental departure from the rule of law as a public, contestable institution. *Opacity is no longer a bug in the system. It is part of the system's design logic.*

This becomes evident when examining how proprietary legal technologies are deployed in practice. In criminal justice, tools like COMPAS or the Public Safety Assessment have been adopted to aid in sentencing, parole, and bail decisions. These systems generate risk scores based on historical data—often including prior arrests, age, employment status, and other socio-economic variables. The algorithms themselves are typically protected under trade secret law, meaning neither defence attorneys nor the defendants themselves are granted access to the model's internal logic. When challenged, vendors and courts have routinely prioritised intellectual property protections over the defendant's right to understand the basis of a decision that may affect their liberty. *The institutional norm of legal transparency is overridden by a commercial norm of competitive secrecy.*

This situation is not the result of poorly drafted procurement contracts or naive optimism about new technology. It reflects a deliberate structuring of opacity as a competitive advantage. Legal-tech vendors routinely promote their tools as proprietary innovations whose efficacy depends on unique data access, complex modelling, and secret optimisation techniques. Their business models depend on exclusivity. In many cases, even the public agencies licensing these tools are restricted from auditing them independently. Systemic review, algorithmic auditing, and source code inspection are blocked not because they are impossible, but because they are seen as commercially hazardous. Courts and governments become both users and dependents—locked into systems they do not fully control, unable to explain or contest how outcomes are derived.

The contradiction could not be sharper. Legal systems demand that decisions be explainable. A judge must offer written reasoning. A prosecutor must justify a charge. A public body must account for its actions under administrative law. Yet AI systems used in these very contexts are often incapable of explanation—or rather, designed to be unexplainable in meaningful human terms. Deep learning models, in particular, generate outputs from millions of parameter interactions that are not intuitively intelligible. Attempts at post hoc explainability—such as SHAP values or LIME visualisations—may offer statistical correlations, but they do not replicate the kind of normative reasoning that undergirds legal argument. And where simpler models might be more interpretable, vendors often resist using them for fear of compromising competitive performance. In this sense, opacity is *strategic*. It is not the result of technological maturity lagging behind social need; it is the outcome of a market logic that treats visibility as liability.

This problem is not confined to criminal justice. In commercial law, automated contract analysis tools are increasingly relied upon for due diligence, risk flagging, and standard clause detection. These platforms—many of which leverage unsupervised or semi-supervised machine learning—advertise their speed and coverage as superior to human review. But clients are rarely informed about the datasets on which these systems were trained, the heuristics used to define "risk," or the criteria for flagging anomalous language. In legal practice, where accountability depends on traceable reasoning and defendable judgment, such tools introduce a new form of hidden delegation. A clause may be marked as "non-standard," triggering negotiation delays or fee adjustments, without any clear indication of why it was marked, what assumptions underlie the classification, or how the result compares across jurisdictions. *The algorithm speaks with authority, but not with accountability.*

The opacity of these systems also functions as a shield against bias accountability. Many legal-tech vendors argue that disclosing their training data, feature weights, or decision criteria would expose them to criticism about discriminatory outcomes. By keeping these components opaque, they avoid public debate about how their models may reinforce racial, gender, or socio-economic disparities. Bias, if acknowledged at all, is addressed through general assurances—promises that the data was "cleaned," that fairness metrics were applied, or that the outputs were independently validated. Yet without access to the model's structure and data provenance, such assurances are unverifiable. Bias mitigation becomes a marketing claim, not a matter of public trust. *Opacity enables not just commercial protection, but epistemic impunity.*

Even regulatory frameworks designed to ensure fairness struggle against the deliberate construction of black-box systems. In the EU, the General Data Protection Regulation (GDPR) includes a right to "meaningful information about the logic involved" in automated decisions. In theory, this grants individuals some access to the reasoning behind algorithmic determinations. In practice, however, this provision has been interpreted narrowly, and often sidestepped by defining outputs as "recommendations" rather than final decisions. If a judge, administrator, or officer signs off on a machine-generated result—even perfunctorily—the decision is reclassified as human, thereby avoiding the legal obligations tied to automated processing. This creates a façade of human oversight, while preserving the underlying opacity of the machine logic. *Transparency is maintained in form, not in substance.*

What makes this issue especially troubling is the growing institutional dependence on such systems. Courts facing backlogs, agencies under budgetary pressure, and firms seeking cost efficiency are increasingly turning to AI tools not just for support but for substitution. As reliance deepens, the incentive to scrutinise decreases. Decisions that once required debate are now made silently by systems whose inner workings no one in the room fully understands. Judges defer to scores. Officers follow flagging systems. Lawyers outsource triage to platforms. Over time, what was introduced as a convenience becomes infrastructure—and the infrastructure is opaque by design. *Legal actors become procedural intermediaries to machine-generated decisions, rather than sources of judgment themselves.*

Calls for greater transparency are often countered by concerns about security, manipulation, or gaming the system. If algorithms were fully disclosed, the argument goes, bad actors could exploit them. But this framing elides the distinction between operational secrecy and institutional opacity. It is possible to provide meaningful access, auditability, and procedural explanation without revealing every line of code or data record. Human decision-makers are expected to justify their reasoning without being rendered vulnerable to manipulation; algorithmic systems should be held to a similar standard. The issue is not whether every technical detail must be disclosed—it is whether affected individuals and oversight bodies have the tools and authority to understand, contest, and improve the systems in question.

The deeper philosophical problem is that opacity, once normalised, reshapes the expectations of legal decision-making. It encourages a view of law as output rather than process, as score rather than reason. It treats judgment as the application of optimised rules, not the weighing of competing principles. Over time, this erodes the culture of justification that underpins democratic legal systems. The commitment to reason-giving—to showing one's work, to standing behind a decision—is replaced by a commitment to performance metrics and system calibration. This is not progress. It is *an abdication of the legal system's ethical commitment to transparency, contestability, and reasoned authority.*

To treat opacity as an inevitable by-product of AI in law is to surrender too easily. We must name it for what it often is: a feature built to protect commercial advantage, suppress public scrutiny, and avoid hard conversations about bias and responsibility. If legal systems are to retain their legitimacy in an age of algorithmic governance, they must resist the silent drift toward unaccountable automation. They must insist that every tool used to shape rights, obligations, or freedoms be visible to those it governs. Not because transparency is a silver bullet, but because *without it, law becomes indistinguishable from administration—and justice indistinguishable from convenience.*

Whose Judgment Counts?

A machine does not form convictions. It does not weigh sorrow, history, or remorse. It does not flinch at human suffering, nor does it stand humbled before a complex moral dilemma. Yet, increasingly, algorithmic systems are making decisions that carry the full weight of judgment. Bail recommendations, sentencing guidelines, hiring suitability, eligibility for asylum—these determinations, once the province of judges, advocates, and juries, are being shaped, accelerated, or outright rendered by software. The shift is not just technological; it is existential. It forces a redefinition of whose reasoning matters—and whose values are silently embedded in the tools we now use to deliver justice.

Every legal decision contains an implicit narrative about what matters: which facts are salient, which principles apply, which outcomes are just. These narratives have traditionally been debated, reasoned, and recorded in courtrooms and legal documents—environments built for transparency, challenge, and evolution. But algorithmic systems do not narrate. They compute. They reduce vast social complexity to inputs and outputs, feature weights and thresholds, probability scores and classifications. The danger is not merely that this process oversimplifies. It is that it conceals the moral and cultural assumptions embedded within it. *When a machine decides, whose judgment does it reflect—and who authorised that reflection?*

Take the example of COMPAS, one of the most widely known risk assessment tools used in the United States to evaluate the likelihood of recidivism. Although marketed as an objective tool, investigations have revealed that its predictions can differ along racial lines, with Black defendants often rated as higher risk than white defendants with similar criminal histories. The developers deny racial bias, arguing that the algorithm optimises for general accuracy. But that defence only raises a deeper question: *accuracy according to whose metric, calibrated against which social truths, and prioritising which consequences?* An algorithm may not intend to discriminate, but it inevitably reflects the societal structures, historical data, and engineering priorities on which it is built.

That reflection is not neutral. The choice of training data encodes a vision of what has counted as crime, deviance, or credibility in the past. The modelling decisions—what counts as a relevant variable, what weights to assign, which correlations to trust—encode judgments about causality, responsibility, and trustworthiness. The optimisation goals—whether to minimise false positives, reduce case processing time, or improve conviction rates—encode priorities about efficiency versus fairness, risk versus redemption. In every step of the pipeline, human value decisions are encoded as technical design. But unlike a judge's written opinion, they are rarely named, explained, or subjected to adversarial challenge. *The human element does not disappear—it is buried beneath the surface, inaccessible and unaccountable.*

Even in ostensibly mundane domains, such as contract analysis or compliance review, the same pattern holds. AI systems used by law firms and corporations to scan NDAs, procurement documents, or employment agreements make assumptions about what constitutes "risk," "non-standard terms," or "problematic language." These assumptions are not inherently wrong, but they are shaped by the developers' legal culture, the preferences of early clients, and the statistical properties of historical datasets. A clause flagged as risky may be so not because it violates the law or exposes liability, but because it deviates from what a vendor's model was trained to consider "normal." And yet that flag may prompt a lawyer to reject the clause, renegotiate the term, or escalate the contract—all without ever examining the underlying logic. *A decision is made, a judgment is executed, but whose interpretive lens is being applied?*

This raises profound questions about agency, responsibility, and the limits of delegation. In democratic legal systems, legitimacy arises from public visibility and procedural participation. We grant judges the authority to decide because they are appointed or elected through transparent processes, bound by rules of evidence, and required to provide justifications. Their authority is derivative—earned through accountability, appealability, and institutional tradition. But what about an AI system developed by a private vendor, trained on proprietary data, and licensed under commercial confidentiality? It has no public mandate, no duty to explain, no face to hold responsible. Yet it may influence decisions that affect life and liberty.

Can such a system ever be said to judge in any morally or legally meaningful sense?

This is not an abstract concern. In multiple jurisdictions, algorithmic systems are now being consulted in parole decisions, immigration screenings, welfare eligibility, and even child custody assessments. Often these systems are used to "support" human decision-makers, but in practice, their outputs carry presumptive authority. Judges and caseworkers defer to them, sometimes without real understanding of how the results were generated. This deference is not irrational; it reflects institutional pressures—caseloads, time constraints, lack of technical training. But it creates a structural inversion: the machine, initially introduced to augment judgment, begins to displace it. *The system does not ask, "What is just?" It asks, "What does the model say?"*

Compounding the issue is the fragmentation of accountability. When a questionable decision is made on the basis of AI output, responsibility becomes diffuse. The judge blames the system. The vendor blames the data. The programmer blames the client. The client blames the procurement process. No one owns the values that guided the decision. No one is empowered to revise them. *This diffusion of accountability is not a by-product of complexity—it is a failure of institutional design.*

To reclaim meaningful judgment in the age of AI, we must confront the uncomfortable reality that no algorithm is value-free. Even the choice to optimise for "accuracy" over "equity," or "efficiency" over "due process," reflects a prioritisation of some social goods over others. These priorities are not technical—they are moral. They deserve the same level of debate, scrutiny, and contestation that we demand from human judges and legislators. The central issue is not whether AI can make accurate decisions. It is whether the values embedded in those decisions are visible, negotiable, and democratically legitimate.

And yet, in many current deployments, those values are not only invisible—they are unknowable. Models developed under commercial confidentiality often withhold training data, model architecture, and even error rates. Vendors claim this secrecy is necessary to protect intellectual property or prevent system gaming.

But the effect is to remove decisions from public contestability. *If we cannot question the basis of a judgment, we cannot meaningfully appeal it. If we cannot appeal it, we are no longer living under a system of law, but a system of administered outputs.*

This shift is subtle but seismic. It replaces the human-centred ethic of judgment—with all its imperfections, deliberations, and moral weight—with a machinic logic of prediction and classification. It swaps the courtroom's ethos of argument for the machine's promise of statistical confidence. What gets lost in the process is not just the texture of individual cases, but the very idea that law is something we reason through together. *To accept machine-generated decisions without interrogating whose judgment they encode is to surrender not just authority, but agency.*

In the end, the most important question is not whether AI can judge, but whether we are still willing to. Are we prepared to define which principles matter, who gets to enshrine them, and how they must be defended? Or will we allow those definitions to be imported silently through code—designed elsewhere, evaluated nowhere, and accepted everywhere? *Whose judgment counts is not just a philosophical inquiry. It is a democratic imperative.*

Chapter 3
Law's Uncodifiable Core

There are statutes, and then there is justice. A society may boast meticulously drafted codes, courts equipped with sophisticated case-management systems, and algorithms capable of predicting risk with uncanny speed. Yet no aggregation of written rules or digital precision can supplant the moral labour inherent in interpretation. The law's wording rarely exhausts its meaning, and that meaning is inseparable from the tangled realities of human life—its motives, contradictions, and wounds. At the heart of any legal system that claims legitimacy lies a constellation of values that stubbornly resist reduction to data points or decision trees.

This is not merely a philosophical claim; it is a structural fact. No algorithm, however sophisticated, can sustain the functioning of a legal system on syntax alone. Legislators do not merely encode prescriptions; they gesture towards ideals. Judges do not simply enforce rules; they weigh equities, read between silences, discern intent. Citizens are not static datasets; they arrive with histories, contexts, and consequences. In every courtroom, boardroom, and bureaucratic setting where law is enacted, one finds interpretation—anchored in empathy, reasoning, memory, and moral imagination. To assume that law can be fully codified, and thus fully computable, is to misunderstand what law is at its core.

Consider the oft-cited, rarely resolved distinction between the letter and the spirit of the law. The letter dictates what must or must not occur; the spirit interrogates why the rule exists, what justice it is meant to serve, and how its application might need adjustment in shifting circumstances. These dimensions rarely coincide neatly. Legal history abounds with cases where rigid adherence to the text would have produced injustice, unless a judge tempered it with moral discernment or societal understanding.

Take, for instance, *Riggs v. Palmer* (1889). A grandson, anxious to secure his inheritance, murdered his grandfather. By a narrow reading, the law might have allowed him to benefit. The court, however, intervened, declaring that "no one shall be permitted to profit by his own fraud." This was not a calculation of clauses; it was moral reasoning in action. Law had to mean more than what it said.

This is precisely the type of interpretive act AI is not designed to perform. Machine-learning models excel at pattern recognition, probabilistic inference, and rule application. They do not apprehend intent, understand purpose, or recognise when a rule should yield to a higher value. An AI might flag a clause as unusual or a case as high risk, but it cannot ask whether the law ought to bend, defer, or yield in pursuit of justice. Nor can it recognise when statutes themselves are tainted by historical bias, discrimination, or systemic inequity.

This limitation is not incidental—it strikes at the very heart of legal reasoning. Law is not mathematics. It is not a closed corpus awaiting computation. It is a normative enterprise unfolding over time through conflict, dissent, adaptation, and repair. To reason legally is not merely to apply rules but to inhabit them—to navigate the spaces where doctrine meets circumstance, where precedent intersects with progress. A system blind to this terrain may yield efficient outputs, yet fail utterly to deliver justice.

In its pursuit of scalable "solutions," Silicon Valley often treats ambiguity as a bug rather than a feature of democratic governance. Contract-analysis software and sentencing algorithms are frequently framed as remedies for inconsistency and subjectivity. Yet legal ambiguity is not noise; it is a vital condition for nuance. It allows judges to weigh mitigating circumstances, account for evolving norms, exercise clemency, and dissent. It is what permits the law to breathe.

Many of the most transformative legal developments have emerged precisely from such ambiguity. Recognition of marital rape, expanded asylum protections, and the legal status of same-sex partnerships arose not from mechanical statute reading but from moral argument, social struggle, and the interpretive courage of those who understood that law must respond, not merely compute.

This responsiveness rests on capacities beyond AI's reach: empathy, judgment, narrative reasoning. A judge can absorb not only the facts of a survivor's testimony but its emotional weight. A lawyer can advocate by invoking the life story that gives a claim its force. A jury can be persuaded not by statistics but by moral recognition. These are not irrational forces; they are central to legal reasoning. Justice emerges through deliberation, compassion, and principled discretion, not from dispassionate calculation.

The current discourse around AI in law tends to privilege computational performance over these human dimensions. But ignoring them risks hollowing out legal practice. A predictive sentencing tool may appear statistically sound, yet it cannot factor in remorse, rehabilitation, or the transformative effects of time. A contract bot may flag deviations from industry norms, but it cannot understand when such deviations are deliberate, relational, or corrective of historical wrongs. Here, what looks like error may be precisely what carries meaning.

This is not to suggest that AI has no role. Judiciously applied, it can streamline routine tasks, improve access to information, and detect patterns beyond human capacity. But its use must be constrained by recognition of what only humans can do. Delegating legal judgment to machines without preserving interpretive oversight is abdication, converting law from a moral institution into a computational service.

The pressing question is not whether AI can "do" law, but whether we are willing to defend what law truly is. Are we prepared to insist that justice requires more than consistency—that it demands moral vision, context sensitivity, and ethical discretion? Are we ready to protect those zones of ambiguity where human values are negotiated, not programmed? Can we resist the lure of certainty when that certainty comes at the expense of understanding?

These questions arise in concrete ways: whenever parole boards defer to risk scores, hiring decisions are automated, or predictive policing informs interventions. They arise whenever the spirit of the law is displaced by algorithmic conformity—and their urgency will only grow as computational logic permeates legal practice.

At stake is not merely the integrity of legal systems but the character of the societies they serve. A legal system incapable of recognising moral intent, weighing human complexity, or tolerating discretion is not just flawed—it is unfit for justice. Law's uncodifiable core is not a technical inconvenience; it is a democratic safeguard, shielding society from the tyranny of both state and algorithm.

To forget this is to risk building systems that are procedurally immaculate yet substantively blind. The challenge ahead is to modernise tools without mechanising judgment, to steward law not only as text but as a living moral practice, and to ask with each new deployment of legal technology not only what it can do, but what it must never be permitted to replace.

Morality, Context, and Intent

A legal system that cannot reckon with intent ceases to be a moral enterprise. It becomes, instead, a bureaucratic machine—one capable of sorting facts and applying codes, but unable to ask the most human of questions: *Why did this happen? What did the actor mean to do? What should justice look like here, not merely what the rule requires?* At the heart of legal interpretation lies the effort to make sense of actions in moral and contextual terms—not simply to categorise conduct, but to evaluate it. This capacity is not incidental to law; it is its core. And yet, it is precisely this capacity that artificial intelligence systems lack.

Intent is not an observable quantity. It does not reside in metadata or emerge from probabilities. It must be inferred, constructed, debated—often with reference to tone, history, motive, contradiction, or remorse. When a defendant claims an act was accidental, or a legislator writes a vaguely worded statute, or a witness equivocates under pressure, it is not the literal wording or factual record alone that guides judgment. It is the human act of interpretation—an act that draws on experience, empathy, and moral frameworks that no machine has.

Consider how the law approaches murder. The same physical act—killing another person—may be punished differently based on intent. Was it premeditated? Was it committed in a moment of passion? Was it an accident, an act of defence, or something else entirely? The difference between first-degree murder and manslaughter is not in what occurred, but in *why* it occurred. Legal systems recognise that *motive matters*, that the *mental state* of an actor is not merely relevant but determinative. Yet AI, trained on patterns in data, cannot perceive mental states. It can only approximate likelihoods.

This limitation is not merely technical; it is structural. Statistical models are designed to *correlate*, not to *understand*. They identify patterns in past behaviour to make predictions about future actions. But law does not treat humans as predictable inputs. It treats them as moral agents. The legal doctrine of *mens rea*—the "guilty mind"—exists precisely because we believe that culpability requires not just an act, but a certain intention behind it. *Intent transforms a fact pattern into a legal meaning.*

And this legal meaning is rarely straightforward. The process by which intent is assessed is often layered and contested. Judges weigh conflicting narratives. Lawyers frame motive through character, context, and consequences. Juries are asked not just to process information, but to evaluate *credibility*. In many cases, ambiguity is not a problem to be resolved, but a reality to be deliberated. Justice does not demand certainty—it demands care, discernment, and principled judgment.

This is where AI, for all its processing power, cannot follow. It lacks the ability to reason morally. A machine can model risk, but it cannot model remorse. It can flag anomalies, but it cannot understand meaning. It may recognise that a term in a contract deviates from industry standards, but it cannot determine whether that deviation was an act of exploitation or an act of generosity. It lacks *normative literacy*—the capacity to interpret not just what happened, but *what it signifies within a human framework of justice.*

Take the example of employment discrimination. Suppose an AI system is tasked with flagging unfair hiring practices based on historical data. The patterns it identifies may reflect bias—but also, paradoxically, may be *shaped by* that same bias. If a firm has systematically undervalued applicants from certain schools or regions, the system may learn that these applicants are "less successful." In such a case, the machine's interpretation is not neutral—it is the product of a flawed moral history. But unlike a human reviewer, the system cannot *recognise* that the data reflects injustice. It simply replicates it, unintentionally reinforcing the very harm it was deployed to reduce.

Legal interpretation often requires *reading against the grain*—seeing not just what the data shows, but what it conceals. This is especially true in cases involving historical trauma or structural inequality. Statutes may appear facially neutral while having discriminatory effects. Precedents may have been shaped in unjust eras. A judge aware of these dynamics might interpret a rule narrowly, or decline to follow a precedent altogether. An AI system, in contrast, lacks any sense of history, memory, or ethical caution. *It does not know what it does not know.*

This blindness extends to legislative intent. When courts interpret statutes, they often consult legislative history—not merely the text, but the debates, reports, and stated purposes behind the law. These sources help reveal what lawmakers hoped to achieve, what compromises were made, and how ambiguities should be resolved. But such interpretive work is not reducible to a single vector or score. It requires reading tone, considering context, understanding political subtext. It is, in essence, a form of moral archaeology. *AI cannot conduct such archaeology because it does not understand purpose.*

Nor can it understand irony, subtext, or strategic ambiguity—tools often deliberately employed by lawmakers or negotiators to accommodate competing interests. Legal actors routinely leave room for interpretation, knowing that future contexts may demand flexibility. Ambiguity is not always a flaw. It is often a recognition that justice cannot be exhaustively specified in advance. But this kind of purposeful vagueness is precisely what machine logic struggles to process. AI demands specification. The human legal mind, by contrast, tolerates—and often requires—interpretive openness.

This raises profound risks when AI is used in settings that hinge on ethical nuance. Automated sentencing recommendations, parole risk assessments, or child welfare determinations are not just administrative tasks—they are deeply moral judgments. They require attention to life histories, social dynamics, and the intangible quality of human suffering. Delegating such decisions to systems that cannot perceive suffering or comprehend rehabilitation is not efficient—it is dehumanising. *It flattens moral evaluation into mathematical optimisation.*

The problem is not merely that machines cannot assess intent. It is that their very design discourages it. The architecture of most machine learning systems rewards precision, not ambiguity; efficiency, not empathy. As such, these systems tend to exclude moral complexity by default. The training data lacks context, the objective functions ignore values, and the interpretive layer is absent. What emerges is not a tool for justice, but a calculator of conformity.

To illustrate, consider predictive policing tools. These systems forecast where crimes are likely to occur based on past reports. But they do not account for *why* certain areas are policed more heavily, or why some communities are more likely to be reported than others. The model identifies correlations, but offers no insight into structural causes. It cannot ask whether the patterns it detects are the result of discrimination, poverty, or over-surveillance. Nor can it propose solutions rooted in dignity or social repair. It can only propose *more policing*. In this way, *the absence of moral reasoning becomes a mechanism of moral failure.*

What then, is the path forward? It is not to reject technology outright, but to recognise its limits. AI can assist in legal tasks—organising documents, identifying inconsistencies, flagging anomalies—but it should never be the final arbiter of intent or morality. Legal systems must preserve interpretive space for humans to deliberate, dissent, and reflect. They must resist the urge to automate judgment simply because judgment is difficult. And they must affirm, at every turn, that *understanding intent is not optional in justice—it is justice.*

The promise of the rule of law lies not in its rigidity, but in its responsiveness. In its capacity to hear not just what was said, but what was meant. Not just what occurred, but what was intended. Not just what is efficient, but what is *right.* This promise cannot be delivered by code alone. It demands presence, wisdom, and moral attention. It demands us.

The Spirit vs. The Letter

When courts adjudicate disputes, they do so not merely by applying words, but by interpreting meanings. Yet in a system increasingly nudged toward automation—where algorithms parse statutes like computer code and legal outcomes are predicted by probabilistic models—this distinction between the *spirit* and the *letter* of the law is not just semantic. It is existential.

The law is not a fixed set of instructions to be executed with mechanical precision; it is a living system animated by context, guided by ethics, and shaped by cultural evolution. At its heart lies a fundamental tension: should justice be rendered through the strict application of codified text, or by understanding the broader intention behind it? This question predates AI, but artificial intelligence makes it impossible to ignore. For the first time, we are delegating decisions with moral and social weight to systems that do not, and cannot, grasp human meaning.

Consider the case of *Holy Trinity Church v. United States* (1892), often cited in American legal education. A statute barred the importation of foreign labourers under contract. A literal reading included a church's hiring of a foreign pastor. But the U.S. Supreme Court ruled otherwise, holding that the spirit of the law intended to curb manual labour contracts that exploited immigrant workers—not to target clergy. The Court famously declared, "A thing may be within the letter of the statute and yet not within its spirit." That single sentence captures the core dilemma: meaning is not reducible to syntax. A machine may recognise textual match, but it cannot understand legislative purpose unless it is pre-programmed or inferred by proxies—both limited stand-ins for human discernment.

This conflict is not confined to arcane or historical cases. Contemporary examples abound. In the United Kingdom, the 2019 Supreme Court ruling in R *(Miller) v The Prime Minister* is illustrative. The Court held that the Prime Minister's advice to the Queen to prorogue Parliament was unlawful. Nowhere in constitutional text was such action explicitly barred; but the spirit of constitutional principles—parliamentary sovereignty and democratic accountability—demanded judicial intervention. An AI system, trained solely on written precedent or statute, would struggle to even frame the legal question, let alone resolve it. It could not intuit that the real issue was not the act of prorogation itself, but its effect on democratic legitimacy.

Legal practitioners rely heavily on precedent, but they do not treat prior decisions as mere templates. They ask: was the ruling just? Was it appropriate to the facts? Was it fair in context? AI systems trained on legal corpora absorb patterns but not principles. They detect statistical regularities in outcomes, but cannot ask why a rule was bent or a dissent was persuasive. They do not learn that sometimes *not* applying the rule is itself the highest expression of law. The flexibility of human judgment—its ability to deviate from form without abandoning fidelity—is what breathes life into the law. Algorithmic rigidity, however elegant, cannot replicate that nuance.

Moreover, the spirit-letter divide becomes even more acute when interpreting ambiguous or contested terms. What does "reasonable force" mean in self-defence? What constitutes "undue influence" in contract law? These are not concepts with hard edges. They require a reader who understands not only what was said, but what was meant. Judges draw upon shared cultural understanding, evolving social norms, and competing moral theories. AI has no moral theory. It lacks a theory of mind. Its "understanding" is pattern recognition, not principle application.

One might argue that algorithmic law could be made more sophisticated by encoding legislative intent or incorporating judicial philosophy. But intent is not always legible or agreed upon. Parliament rarely speaks with one voice. Judges often disagree sharply on interpretive method—textualism, purposivism, originalism—each yielding different outcomes from the same provision. Whose philosophy should be encoded? And who decides when the machine must deviate from past form to uphold future justice?

This is not a speculative concern. AI systems are already deployed in legal domains that require interpretive flexibility. In the United States, tools like COMPAS assess the risk of reoffending to guide bail and sentencing. Their developers claim neutrality, but studies have shown racially biased outputs. Why? Because the model follows the letter of its training data, not the spirit of equal protection. In essence, it mimics precedent without moral memory. No algorithm flagged that it was perpetuating historical injustice. No line of code hesitated before treating prior arrests as an objective measure of future risk.

Or take contract analysis software. Many platforms can now parse thousands of clauses in seconds, identifying deviations from standard templates. But when a clause is novel or context-dependent—say, a force majeure clause invoking pandemic-related supply chain failures—the tool may flag it as non-compliant, even if it reflects reasonable adaptation. Machines excel at pattern conformity, but struggle with purposeful deviation. They can detect difference but not always justify why difference might matter.

In some circles, especially in the tech industry, the desire for "clean" data has led to a push for eliminating ambiguity altogether. The view is that if the law were just better codified—if it were more like code—then machines could execute it flawlessly. But this betrays a deep misunderstanding. Ambiguity is not a bug in the legal system; it is a feature. It allows the law to adapt without constant revision. It allows judges to consider the unforeseeable. It enables equity to temper excess.

This interpretive openness is not a flaw in need of machine correction. It is the scaffolding of justice. Codifying every possibility invites either suffocating rigidity or dangerous overreach. Human interpreters—fallible, biased, and inconsistent though they may be—offer something algorithms cannot: the capacity to wrestle with meaning as a moral and cultural act.

To claim that AI will someday "understand" legal meaning is to conflate simulation with cognition. Yes, it may approximate outcomes in well-structured cases. But where rules are stretched, where precedents conflict, where justice demands departure from the past, the spirit must guide the decision. And that spirit is irreducibly human.

None of this is to suggest that AI has no role in law. On the contrary, it has already proved invaluable in discovery, document review, and even compliance tracking. But these functions are primarily operational, not interpretive. They assist with execution, not judgment. The danger lies in allowing their precision to seduce us into outsourcing discernment. Law without context is code. And justice without understanding is compliance without conscience.

If we are to preserve the dignity of legal interpretation, we must resist the temptation to treat machines as judges. We must design with humility, deploy with caution, and legislate with wisdom. Because the letter of the law, on its own, cannot dispense justice. It is the spirit—messy, moral, and magnificently human—that makes the law worthy of our trust.

Discretion as a Feature, Not a Flaw

The most unsettling misunderstanding Silicon Valley brings to the legal domain is the belief that discretion is a defect. In a worldview shaped by data engineering and software development, ambiguity is error, vagueness is inefficiency, and interpretation is noise that should be eliminated in favour of consistency and scale. But in law, these very elements—discretion, ambiguity, and context—are not failings to be debugged. They are among the few mechanisms through which justice breathes.

Legal discretion is often portrayed as a threat to fairness: the unpredictable variable that opens the door to human bias, error, or favouritism. The tech industry, drawing from this narrative, has sold algorithmic neutrality as the antidote. On its surface, the pitch is seductive—replace partial human judgment with impartial computational logic. But this framing obscures a crucial truth: *discretion is not the problem; misused discretion is.* In capable hands, discretion allows a judge to account for individual circumstance, to recognise when a strict application of the rule would produce an unjust outcome. It allows the law to see the person before it, not just the precedent behind them.

Contrast that with the dominant engineering culture of artificial intelligence. In machine learning systems, clarity is king. Data must be labelled, input-output relationships must be defined, and ambiguity must be resolved in advance. There is no room for lingering intent, for moral tension, for the intuition that something doesn't fit even if it formally checks all the boxes. The system will do what it was optimised to do, and only that. When applied to legal decision-making, this architecture becomes more than a technical limitation—it becomes an ethical failure.

Consider immigration adjudications. Two asylum seekers from the same country, facing comparable dangers, may differ meaningfully in age, mental health, or the trauma endured on their journey. A good judge does not flatten these nuances. They weigh them. They allow these qualitative aspects to inform judgment without being reducible to a decision tree. But when case assessments are fed into algorithmic tools—such as automated risk classifiers now trialled in parts of the US immigration system—the richness of discretion is replaced by quantifiable proxies: country of origin, prior arrest records, employment history. The applicant becomes a datapoint, not a life.

The clean-data mindset rejects messiness because messiness is difficult to automate. But *law is inherently messy.* Its legitimacy derives not from binary outcomes but from deliberative processes—ones that can tolerate complexity, dissent, and even contradiction. In courtrooms, ambiguity is not merely accepted; it is explored. Legal training revolves around parsing grey zones, interpreting statutory intent, and weighing precedent in light of changing norms. There is no universal function that takes legal inputs and returns a correct answer—because what counts as "correct" in law is always mediated by values.

This is what predictive AI fails to grasp. Trained on historical outcomes, it learns the patterns of what *was* decided, not what *ought to have been* decided. It optimises for likelihood, not justice. Tools like COMPAS, used to forecast recidivism, were built on such logic. They were supposed to guide sentencing with objectivity, but their predictions baked in the biases of their data—penalising black defendants based on historical arrest disparities, not any individualised wrongdoing. The systems operated with mechanical consistency, but without moral judgment. They were precise in the way a spreadsheet is precise: indifferent to the consequences of their own logic.

It's not only in sentencing or asylum that discretion matters. In family law, discretion allows a judge to weigh the best interests of a child beyond financial means or visitation checklists. In employment tribunals, it enables context-specific analysis of discrimination claims. In criminal trials, it allows for mercy—something no statistical model can compute. To strip discretion from these processes is not to make them fairer. It is to make them blind to the very principles they claim to uphold.

Indeed, legal systems have long relied on ambiguity as a form of resilience. Loosely defined standards—such as "reasonable doubt," "good faith," or "due care"—are intentionally open to interpretation. They are not bugs in the legal code; they are placeholders for moral reasoning. They invite argument, deliberation, and evolution. They reflect a trust in human judgment to fill in the interpretive gaps based on cultural context and changing societal expectations.

But when AI is tasked with interpreting these standards, the pressure to disambiguate becomes overwhelming. The result is a simplification that feels neutral but distorts meaning. Take the concept of "fair use" in intellectual property. It depends on a balancing test—considering purpose, market impact, and originality. No two fair use cases are the same. Yet machine-generated legal summaries often reduce this to a checklist, missing the qualitative judgment central to the doctrine. Similarly, terms like "public interest" or "proportionality" require interpretive discretion that algorithms cannot simulate without collapsing nuance into false equivalence.

This technological pressure toward clarity is not neutral—it is political. It privileges efficiency over justice, predictability over compassion. And it often serves the interests of those designing the systems, not those subjected to their decisions. When legal tech firms sell predictive tools to overburdened courts or administrative agencies, the marketing language is one of streamlining: faster outcomes, fewer errors, more throughput. What is lost is often not measured: the informal negotiations, the backroom deliberations, the sighs of recognition when someone breaks protocol for the sake of mercy.

Such losses are not trivial. They amount to a recoding of the justice system itself. When discretion is algorithmically minimised, outcomes may be more consistent, but they are also more brittle. There is less room for course correction. Less space for ethical doubt. Fewer opportunities for redemption. In short, less humanity.

To reframe discretion as a feature rather than a flaw is not to romanticise its abuses. It is to defend its possibility. Discretion can be reviewed. It can be appealed. It is wielded by humans who are answerable to institutional processes. Algorithmic determinations, by contrast, are often shielded by proprietary opacity and cloaked in the authority of objectivity. The judge who explains a difficult ruling can be questioned. The algorithm that issues a score cannot.

Reclaiming discretion requires resisting the ideology that equates automation with progress. It demands a reassertion of law as a human enterprise—not because humans are always better decision-makers, but because *some kinds of decisions should never be made without us*. Discretion enables law to remain unfinished, adaptable, and humane. It allows us to pause, to reflect, to say, "this time, the rule doesn't fit."

Silicon Valley thrives on problems that can be solved. But justice is not a problem to be solved. It is a condition to be sustained. A system that can tolerate ambiguity, honour difference, and uphold fairness despite complexity is not broken. It is mature. And it is precisely the kind of system we will lose if we continue treating discretion as a flaw to be eliminated, rather than a principle to be defended.

Can Empathy Be Programmed?

In 2016, a Wisconsin man named Eric Loomis was sentenced to six years in prison, in part based on a score generated by a proprietary algorithm called COMPAS. The system had flagged him as high risk—more likely to reoffend—without revealing how it reached that conclusion. When Loomis contested the use of an opaque tool in a decision as life-altering as incarceration, the court upheld the sentence. The algorithm, it seemed, had spoken. But what the COMPAS system never considered—what it *couldn't* consider—was the complexity of Loomis's circumstances, his remorse, or the nuanced human context that might bear upon mercy, rehabilitation, or fairness. It executed a pattern; it did not *listen.*

This is the terrain we now enter: where technologies that can parse vast legal corpora, identify anomalies in tax filings, and flag contract clauses for risk are increasingly asked to perform something far more elusive—legal empathy. Can a machine grasp the tremor in a defendant's voice? Can it understand the significance of intergenerational trauma, or the social weight of systemic bias? Or, more fundamentally, *should* it?

The tension is not merely technical. It is epistemological. Legal empathy is not an accessory to the judicial process—it is a central organ. Judges are not merely logic processors; they are mediators of moral complexity. Their role extends beyond rules into the realm of *understanding*—not just what the law says, but what justice demands.

Empathy, as applied to law, operates at several levels. At sentencing, it allows a judge to contextualise an act of desperation during a period of unemployment rather than reduce it to a statistical crime. In asylum law, it allows an adjudicator to interpret fragmented testimony not as deceit but as evidence of trauma. In family court, it empowers a judge to balance procedure with the best interests of a child, a determination rooted in emotional and social context that defies codification.

AI systems, by contrast, operate in environments of statistical inference. They simulate understanding by learning from historical correlations. But human empathy is not a dataset. It involves moral imagination, perspective-taking, and attunement to a speaker's affect, body language, and cultural context—dimensions machines neither experience nor comprehend. *To replicate empathy computationally is to simulate what has no stable form.*

Consider the recent deployment of AI tools in immigration adjudication. Some proposals advocate for AI to assist in identifying fraudulent asylum claims or to expedite routine approvals. On the surface, this seems practical—many cases involve repeatable patterns and standard evidence. But history warns otherwise. Asylum cases often hinge on fractured narratives, cultural idioms, and accounts of violence too painful to recount fluently. A machine trained on "truthful" past claims may penalise precisely those who cannot conform to the dominant linguistic or emotional script. What appears efficient becomes exclusionary. Empathy, here, is not peripheral—it is protective.

The challenge deepens when we recognise that many current AI tools already shape legal decision-making, albeit indirectly. Predictive policing models disproportionately target communities already over-surveilled, reinforcing cycles of criminalisation. Automated benefits assessments flag applications for fraud based on proxies that correlate more with poverty than deception. These systems, though not judicial in the strict sense, influence access to housing, healthcare, freedom. Yet they do so without accountability, without the reflective pause that empathy demands.

Silicon Valley often conceives of fairness as a data problem: if only we could feed the system better training data—more diverse, more "balanced"—the machine would learn to be just. But *legal empathy is not a function of dataset quality.* It is a relational act. It involves moral deliberation, not optimisation. The assumption that empathy can be reduced to a subroutine betrays a technocratic hubris—a belief that the complexity of human moral life can be compressed into tokens and weights.

And yet, some technologists argue that *simulated* empathy may be better than none at all. In overburdened courts or strained public systems, an algorithm that flags when a person is at risk of being misunderstood—because of linguistic barriers, neurodivergence, or past trauma—might improve outcomes. For instance, natural language processing could detect signs of mental distress in testimony, prompting a human review rather than triggering automatic rejection. Here, AI becomes *an assistant to empathy*, not its replacement. But even in such use cases, the line between augmentation and automation is perilously thin.

There is also the concern of performative empathy—systems designed to *appear* caring without actually caring. Some corporate chatbots already attempt this: "I'm sorry you're feeling this way." These canned responses, while superficially consoling, risk trivialising real emotion. In a legal setting, such simulations might lead users to believe their concerns have been understood when they have merely been categorised. The danger is not just inefficacy—it is deception.

In deliberative systems, *intentional opacity* compounds the problem. Proprietary AI models often shroud their decision-making under intellectual property claims, making it impossible to verify whether any empathetic parameters were encoded—or if such claims are merely a gloss. When a machine issues a denial of benefits or suggests a prison term, who is morally accountable? The developer? The judge who accepted the recommendation? The vendor who licensed the software? In systems that cannot feel, it becomes harder to locate ethical responsibility.

Some scholars have proposed hybrid models—systems that assist human decision-makers by providing statistical baselines, while allowing judges to override them based on moral reasoning. These models acknowledge the limits of algorithmic empathy while still offering efficiencies in low-stakes or high-volume tasks. But such systems depend on judicial resistance to technocratic inertia. Once a baseline is established, how often will judges feel empowered to depart from it, especially if doing so invites scrutiny or delay? The risk is that empathy becomes the *outlier*, not the norm.

The question of whether empathy can be programmed thus resolves into a deeper inquiry: what kind of legal system do we want to build? One that centres fairness as *relational, interpretive, and human*, or one that reduces justice to the efficient application of patterns? The answer is not technological—it is philosophical.

And yet, we must not romanticise human empathy either. Judges are fallible, biased, inconsistent. Some show excessive leniency to those who resemble them, or unwarranted harshness to those who don't. Empathy, in practice, can be skewed by unconscious prejudice. The promise of AI, its advocates argue, is consistency—a safeguard against caprice. But *consistency without context is not justice.* It is bureaucracy.

This is not a rejection of technology, but a call for epistemic humility. If legal empathy is to remain central to justice, we must design systems that *support* it without pretending to replace it. That may mean rejecting the allure of full automation in favour of slower, more deliberative hybrids. It may mean accepting that not all aspects of justice scale. Or that in some cases, *not knowing* is better than pretending to know.

The courtroom, unlike the spreadsheet, is a space of narrative. Of pain articulated and answered. Of silence that must be interpreted, not dismissed. Empathy is what allows law to listen rather than just decide. Until machines can do that—not just parse but *understand*, not just assess but *care*—they should remain tools, not judges. Justice without empathy is efficient. But it is not just.

Chapter 4
Machines as Legal Actors

In January 2023, a small startup named DoNotPay captured headlines by announcing its intention to deploy an AI-driven chatbot to argue a case in a United States courtroom, guiding a defendant in real time via an earpiece. Legal challenges ultimately halted the experiment, but the signal was unmistakable: artificial intelligence is no longer content merely to assist from behind the scenes. It seeks to participate actively, stepping into roles traditionally reserved for human legal actors. The ramifications are significant, not just for the practice of law but for our understanding of professional responsibility, authority, and justice itself.

The legal profession has long been insulated by tradition and regulation. To practise law—as advocate, advisor, or judge—requires extensive training, licensure, and ethical oversight. These measures are more than bureaucratic hurdles; they serve as essential safeguards, ensuring that those exercising legal power do so with competence, accountability, and a commitment to the public good. Now, however, that hierarchy is being inverted: tools once confined to supporting legal reasoning are being marketed as substitutes for lawyers, deployed with minimal transparency or oversight. The machine is no longer a silent assistant; it speaks, and others listen.

This is not hypothetical. AI-generated contracts are executed without human review. Chatbots advise on housing disputes, immigration forms, and consumer complaints. Generative models produce demand letters, wills, and even court filings. In jurisdictions overwhelmed by caseloads or lacking legal aid, the appeal is evident: speed, cost reduction, and accessibility. Yet this apparent liberation carries risks, chief among them the erosion of clarity regarding who is actually providing legal advice and who bears responsibility when that advice proves flawed.

Here emerges what might be called the "Ghost Lawyer" problem: an AI generates legal content, the user acts upon it, and the consequences—sometimes severe—fall entirely upon the individual. Human lawyers can be held accountable through malpractice suits or disciplinary review. Algorithms, by contrast, operate behind layers of corporate disclaimers, technical complexity, and contractual indemnities. The software provider disclaims liability, the client is left without recourse, and the system functions as if service occurred without a responsible actor.

It is tempting to frame this as disruptive innovation. Yet disruption without accountability is not innovation—it is deregulation. Legal practice is far more than a series of repeatable outputs. It is relational, interpretive, and often high-stakes, engaging directly with human lives and societal meaning. Expertise alone does not define a lawyer; ethical obligations constrain how that expertise is exercised. An AI that mimics reasoning without assuming responsibility is, effectively, a rogue participant, displacing both professional guidance and accountability.

The stakes become clearer when we consider what legal representation entails. Representation is not mere information transfer or form completion. It embodies fiduciary duty: acting in the client's best interest, offering honest advice, maintaining confidentiality, and safeguarding rights. It requires judgment—the discernment to know when a situation calls for bespoke advocacy rather than standardised processes. Machines do not possess these capacities. They lack moral posture, institutional embedding, and conscience.

Yet the boundary between assistance and representation is rapidly blurring. When a chatbot suggests legal options, is it informing or advising? When a platform completes court documents based on user input, is it scribing or counselling? Regulators struggle to define the limits. Some advocate licensing AI as legal service providers under new frameworks; others call for outright prohibition in sensitive proceedings. Beneath these debates lies a more fundamental question: can legal representation survive the detachment of work from human responsibility?

DoNotPay offers a telling case study. Initially hailed as the "world's first robot lawyer," the company faced criticism when users reported inaccurate or harmful advice. The CEO lacked legal qualifications, the product was insufficiently vetted, and promotional claims were misleading. A narrative of technological empowerment became a cautionary tale of overreach. Even as DoNotPay stumbled, dozens of similar platforms continue to proliferate, automating small claims, tenant advocacy, and more. Their rise is not anomalous; it marks the new terrain of legal practice.

Underlying this transformation is a fundamental shift in the source of legal authority. Traditionally, legitimacy derived from human credentials: bar membership, oaths, disciplinary record. In the AI era, legitimacy is increasingly judged by functionality: if a machine produces the "right" outcome, does it matter who or what generated it? If a user achieves their desired legal result, must the process be scrutinised? This instrumental lens is tempting—particularly where human lawyers are costly or unavailable—but it is perilous. It reduces law to output, severing it from the ethical and institutional structures that confer moral force.

The societal implications are stark. As AI embeds itself into legal workflows, disparities in access and comprehension may widen. The affluent will retain human lawyers, blending expertise with strategic nuance. Others will rely on automated tools offering only surface-level guidance. A purportedly democratizing technology risks creating a tiered justice system: human advocacy for those who can afford it, automated triage for those who cannot.

Nonetheless, AI is not without merit. It can enhance contract review, legal research, pattern recognition, and preliminary intake. In high-volume, low-risk contexts—traffic violations, simple debt disputes—AI can improve efficiency and access. The crucial task is drawing a principled line between assistance and authority, between tools that inform and those that replace. The former can empower; the latter risk hollowing out the profession they purport to support.

We must reconceive legal AI not as a substitute but as a participant subject to norms: transparency, auditability, responsibility. New frameworks of co-accountability may be required, where humans and machines are jointly answerable for outcomes. Ethical design must hold equal weight with technical sophistication. Regulation should evolve not to stifle innovation but to anchor it in justice.

The question is no longer whether machines will act in legal contexts—they already do. The challenge lies in governing these actions to uphold fairness, transparency, competence, and accountability. We must resist the false dichotomy between Luddism and libertarianism. AI can perform legal work, yes, but it cannot—yet—exercise judgment. Until it can, its role must remain firmly subordinate to human oversight.

Beyond Tools: When AI Performs Legal Work

In a legal dispute filed in San Francisco in 2023, a tenant used an AI-generated demand letter to initiate proceedings against their landlord for unsafe housing conditions. The letter was formatted, cited state statutes, and outlined specific breaches of contract. No lawyer was involved. The platform that created the letter had neither a legal team nor a licence to practise law. Yet its intervention influenced the landlord's response, and the case was settled before it reached court. For the tenant, this was a win. For the legal profession, it raised a more troubling question: *at what point does a tool stop being a tool and start acting as a legal actor?*

The legal profession has long drawn a firm boundary between those authorised to practise law and those who are not. That line has traditionally separated the accountable from the unaccountable, the trained from the amateur, the bound-by-duty from the unsupervised. But that boundary is now eroding—not because non-lawyers are encroaching, but because *non-humans* are. Contract generators, legal chatbots, and AI-powered legal assistants are no longer mere calculators or search engines. Increasingly, they make strategic decisions, draft persuasive arguments, and interact with legal institutions in ways that simulate the role of a human solicitor or advocate. They do not just support legal work—they perform it.

These systems are not merely filling out forms. Many offer real-time analysis, generate tailored legal advice based on user input, and produce communications indistinguishable in tone and substance from those drafted by junior lawyers. Platforms such as Lexion, Spellbook, and Harvey AI are being integrated into major law firms for document automation, due diligence, and internal research. Meanwhile, consumer-facing services like DoNotPay, LawDroid, and Rocket Lawyer provide direct-to-client interfaces that help users draft contracts, fight fines, or challenge bills—without ever speaking to a human lawyer. They function as a sort of quasi-counsel: quick, cheap, and untethered to the usual professional codes.

The seduction of such tools lies in their efficiency. Legal work, particularly in transactional or procedural contexts, often relies on standardisation: a lease agreement, a cease-and-desist letter, a motion to dismiss. AI excels in domains where historical data is abundant and templates abound. The promise is tantalising: *Let the machine do the grunt work. Let the lawyer focus on the strategy.* But as the capabilities of these tools deepen, that division begins to blur. When an AI tool can draft a complex contract clause in seconds—or generate an entire litigation memo based on jurisdictional rules—does the human remain the strategist, or has the locus of judgment quietly shifted?

To many in Silicon Valley, this is not a concern—it's the point. In their view, lawyers are too expensive, too slow, and too wedded to legacy thinking. AI can be trained on millions of cases, legal opinions, and filings. It can replicate style, identify risk, and propose remedies at scale. Why not let algorithms do what lawyers do, better and faster? But this perspective is profoundly ahistorical. Law is not simply the application of rules to facts; it is a human process of reasoning, interpretation, and ethical negotiation. *Legal work, properly understood, is not just technical—it is normative.* It involves weighing competing values, understanding context, and anticipating not just outcomes but consequences. No model, however large, can fully encode that.

Consider the example of an AI tool that drafts a non-disclosure agreement. The output may be syntactically correct, legally valid, and enforceable. But what it cannot do is *advise* on whether an NDA is appropriate in a given context, whether its enforcement might be construed as oppressive, or whether its terms align with the client's long-term interests. Nor can it ask the kind of probing questions a good lawyer might pose: What are you trying to protect? Who will have access to this information? Could the clause you're insisting on backfire later in litigation? These are not technical queries—they are ethical and strategic ones. And they go to the heart of what distinguishes a tool from an actor: *judgment.*

Nevertheless, AI legal tools are already being deployed in ways that demand such judgment. In corporate compliance, AI systems routinely flag potential regulatory breaches based on pattern recognition. In immigration law, platforms screen eligibility for visa categories or asylum applications. In dispute resolution, AI mediators attempt to propose settlements by assessing both parties' preferences. These are not trivial tasks. They require an understanding of not just the rules but their meaning in context. The risk is not that machines make errors—they always will—but that they make errors *no one is empowered or required to catch.*

The danger becomes particularly acute when AI operates at the edge of representation. If a client believes they are receiving legal advice, but the provider disclaims all liability and responsibility, we are entering a grey zone with potentially serious ramifications. Regulators have begun to take notice. In several jurisdictions, bar associations have issued warnings against the unauthorised practice of law by software platforms. Some states in the U.S. have even launched investigations into services that offer what appears to be legal counsel without proper authorisation. But enforcement is slow, and the regulatory frameworks are not designed for non-human actors. *The law still assumes that its agents are people.*

This assumption is becoming harder to maintain. AI systems trained on legal data are increasingly capable of producing outputs that pass muster in courts, contracts, and compliance audits. The gap between simulation and genuine performance is narrowing. When the result "works," clients are less inclined to ask whether the process was proper. But law is not just about results. It is about legitimacy. The legitimacy of a legal process does not rest solely on its efficiency or even its fairness; it rests on *who* is involved, *how* they are empowered, and *to whom* they are accountable. When machines perform legal work, these foundations are quietly rearranged.

The shift also forces us to revisit the professional identity of lawyers. What happens to the legal profession when its entry-level tasks—once a rite of passage for trainees—are automated? If AI handles the first draft of every document, the first pass at legal research, the first step of client intake, what are junior lawyers learning? How will they develop the instincts, the discretion, and the deep context that inform higher-level legal reasoning? The pipeline from apprentice to expert is being disrupted. And while the elimination of drudgery may seem a net good, the long-term erosion of professional formation is not. *You cannot outsource the making of good lawyers to the very tools that displace them.*

This is not to suggest that AI has no place in law. On the contrary, when properly designed, used, and overseen, it can extend legal access, reduce costs, and improve consistency. But it must be integrated in ways that *support* rather than supplant professional responsibility. That means building in transparency, error detection, and escalation pathways to human review. It means clearly distinguishing between systems that *inform* and those that *advise*. And it means resisting the temptation to treat the law as a domain of optimisation, rather than deliberation.

Ultimately, the rise of semi-autonomous legal AI is not just a technological development; it is a philosophical challenge. It forces us to ask: What is the nature of legal authority? Is law merely a system of inputs and outputs, or is it a human institution grounded in values, judgment, and narrative? Can representation be disembodied, or does it require a subject who represents? And if machines are to take on legal roles, what new forms of governance, accountability, and ethical responsibility must we invent?

The answer to these questions will shape the future not only of the legal profession but of justice itself. For if we are not careful, we may find ourselves in a world where legal work is done faster, cheaper, and more pervasively than ever before—yet also more distantly, impersonally, and unaccountably. In such a world, access to law may be broader, but its *meaning* may be hollowed out. The real task, then, is not to ask whether machines *can* perform legal work, but what kind of legal world we are building when they do.

The Ghost Lawyer Problem

A woman in Illinois, unable to afford legal representation for her debt collection case, turned to a well-advertised AI legal chatbot. She entered her story, received what appeared to be a personalised answer citing local statutes, and followed its advice—only to find herself defaulted in court. When she tried to understand why, she discovered there was no lawyer involved, no human oversight, and no recourse for the misleading guidance she had received. The chatbot had generated plausible-sounding advice based on pattern recognition, but it lacked both legal duty and accountability. No one was liable. *The ghost lawyer had spoken—and vanished.*

This is not an isolated story. From contract disputes to immigration forms, a growing number of people are engaging with software that performs what looks, sounds, and functions like legal advice. These AI systems are marketed as tools, assistants, or informational platforms. But when a client interacts with a service that interprets their legal question, analyses jurisdictional rules, and produces a recommended course of action, it is disingenuous to say no advice has been given. *The substance is legal guidance; only the name and responsibility are missing.* Hence the term "ghost lawyer"—an invisible actor dispensing legal opinions without bearing any of the duties traditionally associated with legal practice.

The problem here is not simply one of semantics. The legal profession is built on regulated trust. Solicitors and barristers operate under codes of ethics, fiduciary duties, and licensing requirements. They can be disciplined for misconduct, sued for malpractice, and disbarred for breach of trust. AI systems face no such constraints. They cannot be cross-examined, sanctioned, or held accountable in the same way. This creates a dangerous asymmetry: *real legal consequences are triggered by agents with no legal liability.*

Some defenders argue that AI systems do not truly practise law. They merely provide "information," not "advice." But this distinction collapses under scrutiny. If a user types in their facts and receives an output tailored to their situation—especially one framed in legal language or citing statutory authority—then the line between tool and advisor has already been crossed. The user perceives it as legal counsel, and the system behaves accordingly. Pretending otherwise is a fiction that benefits only the developers and platform owners.

There is also the issue of consent and awareness. Most users of AI legal tools do not understand the underlying mechanisms, assumptions, or limitations of the systems they're using. Terms of service buried in fine print may disclaim liability, assert that no attorney-client relationship is formed, and warn that outputs are "informational only." But these disclaimers are cold comfort when real legal harm results. *If a user acts on faulty advice, the damage is not abstract—it is material, often irreversible, and disproportionately borne by the most vulnerable.*

The ghost lawyer phenomenon is particularly troubling in areas of law where stakes are high and protections are thin. In housing court, tenants rely on AI-generated defences against eviction. In immigration proceedings, asylum seekers consult bots to complete complex paperwork. In consumer disputes, individuals are encouraged to challenge charges, fines, or contract terms using AI-generated letters. These tools can offer real help—but when they err, they do so in silence and without remedy. *There is no malpractice suit to file, no bar association to petition, no formal process for redress.*

Contrast this with the human legal system. Even the most junior solicitor must operate under a duty of candour, a requirement of competence, and an obligation to communicate clearly with clients. They must consider not just what the law says, but how it applies in context. They must weigh risks, consider alternatives, and sometimes advise a client *not* to pursue a certain course, even if it appears superficially viable. AI tools, by contrast, cannot assess client capacity, emotional state, or strategic nuance. They do not caution; they compute.

Some developers, aware of this gap, have begun building hybrid models in which AI tools are supervised or audited by licensed lawyers. This is a welcome development—but it remains rare, expensive, and largely confined to enterprise-level applications. The consumer-facing tools most likely to be used by the legally underserved are also those least likely to offer robust oversight. *In this paradox lies the central irony: those with the least access to real lawyers are most exposed to ghost lawyers.*

This problem is compounded by the opacity of AI systems themselves. Even when developers intend to build safe tools, the complexity of large language models makes it difficult to trace the reasoning behind any specific output. A legal chatbot may draw on millions of data points, but it cannot explain why it chose one precedent over another, or whether it misinterpreted a nuance in local law. It cannot be interrogated for bias, corrected for context, or compelled to revise its understanding. This inscrutability undermines both user trust and legal legitimacy. *A tool that cannot explain itself cannot be held to account.*

Critics of regulation often invoke innovation. They warn that if AI tools are constrained too tightly, access to legal help will be stifled, particularly for those who cannot afford traditional representation. There is truth in this concern. The justice gap is real. Millions navigate legal problems without support, and any tool that widens access is welcome. But access without accountability is not access at all—it is exposure. A system that encourages reliance on unaccountable actors does not serve justice; it merely redistributes risk from the powerful to the precarious.

Some jurisdictions are beginning to act. The American Bar Association has debated the boundaries of unauthorised practice in the context of AI. The United Kingdom's Solicitors Regulation Authority has issued guidance on the use of AI by firms. In Canada and Australia, consumer protection agencies are examining claims made by legal-tech companies. But these efforts remain patchy and reactive. There is no global framework, no consistent definition of what constitutes legal advice in the context of AI, and no clear mechanism for ensuring that ghost lawyers are either domesticated or exposed.

The profession itself must also confront its ambivalence. Many law firms use AI internally to streamline research, generate boilerplate, or assess litigation risk. They rely on the same logic—efficiency, scalability, consistency—that drives consumer-facing tools. But they do so under professional oversight, with human review and institutional accountability. If the legal community values its monopoly on legal advice, it must be willing to define and defend the standards that justify it. *If it cannot explain why human judgment matters, it will be replaced by machines that do not ask permission.*

At the core of the ghost lawyer problem is a deeper philosophical question: *what is legal advice?* Is it merely the matching of facts to rules, or is it the exercise of judgment in uncertain terrain? If it is the former, then machines may well be sufficient. But if it is the latter—as most experienced practitioners would agree—then no algorithm, however sophisticated, can substitute for human counsel. Advice is not just output; it is relationship, responsibility, and risk. And it is these dimensions, not computational capacity, that anchor the practice of law in democratic societies.

In the coming years, we will see more AI systems offering more services, often in more persuasive and personalised ways. The temptation will be to let convenience override caution. But we must resist the illusion that because a system speaks the language of law, it understands the stakes of law. We must insist that anyone who acts like a lawyer—human or machine—be held to the same standards of duty, care, and transparency. Otherwise, we risk building a parallel legal system governed not by rule of law, but by terms of service. In such a system, there will be no face to blame, no hand to shake, and no conscience to appeal to. Only the ghost will remain.

Case Study: DoNotPay and the Automation of Advocacy

In late 2022, DoNotPay—self-described as "the world's first robot lawyer"—made headlines by announcing plans to defend a real defendant in court using artificial intelligence. The idea was simple: the defendant would wear smart glasses and an earpiece, through which an AI-generated script would guide them on what to say in real time during a courtroom proceeding. It was bold, provocative—and legally untenable. When multiple state bar associations threatened criminal prosecution, the company cancelled the trial. What remained was not a breakthrough in legal automation but a cautionary tale about the complexities, boundaries, and ambitions of AI-driven advocacy.

Founded by British entrepreneur Joshua Browder, DoNotPay began in 2015 as a chatbot designed to help users contest parking tickets in London. Its interface was straightforward: users answered a series of structured questions, and the system generated an appeal letter based on templated legal reasoning. Within months, it reportedly helped overturn hundreds of tickets. The allure was instant: justice at the click of a button, especially for those priced out of traditional legal services. But as the platform expanded to cover issues like airline compensation, small claims disputes, landlord-tenant conflicts, and even asylum applications, the stakes—and scrutiny—increased exponentially.

The appeal of DoNotPay rests on a powerful and urgent premise: that legal redress should not be a luxury good. In the United States and United Kingdom alike, legal systems are riddled with structural inequality. Most people cannot afford full representation, and many legal problems—especially civil matters—go unaddressed simply because navigating the system is too complex, expensive, or time-consuming. A service that automates routine filings and demystifies bureaucratic processes speaks directly to this access-to-justice gap. *But when a tool promises more than it can ethically or technically deliver, the very users it aims to empower may become the ones it inadvertently exploits.*

The marketing of DoNotPay often blurs the distinction between legal information and legal representation. While the company insists that it is not a law firm and does not offer legal advice, its claims frequently suggest otherwise. Browder has asserted that DoNotPay can write legal briefs, negotiate settlements, and "replace lawyers." Such declarations are not just bravado; they carry consequences. When consumers believe they are being represented, but are in fact receiving unsupervised machine-generated output, the risks are tangible: missed deadlines, invalid filings, and, in the worst cases, irreparable legal harm. *Automated empowerment becomes automated endangerment.*

A central issue in assessing the ethics and efficacy of DoNotPay is the question of competence. In regulated legal professions, competence is not a marketing slogan—it is a licensure requirement. A solicitor or barrister must demonstrate mastery of the law, uphold professional standards, and accept responsibility for errors. When a chatbot drafts a legal document, who reviews it for jurisdictional relevance, procedural accuracy, or interpretive soundness? The system may mimic legal reasoning, but it lacks the capacity to understand context, nuance, or the client's best interest. Without human oversight, there is no backstop—only the illusion of expertise.

Consider the 2023 class action lawsuit filed against DoNotPay in California. The plaintiff alleged that the company was engaged in the unauthorised practice of law by providing legal services without a license. The complaint argued that users had been misled into thinking they were receiving competent legal assistance, when in fact they were being served auto-generated forms assembled by an AI system with no legal training or liability. Whether or not the case succeeds, it underscores a growing concern: *when does the simulation of advocacy become its unethical substitute?*

Beyond questions of legal compliance lie deeper questions of equity. Who benefits from AI-powered advocacy, and who bears its risks? In theory, tools like DoNotPay are designed for those who cannot afford traditional counsel—tenants facing eviction, workers denied wages, consumers defrauded by corporations. But these are precisely the individuals least equipped to evaluate the reliability of automated advice. They often lack legal literacy, digital fluency, or the resources to pursue redress if something goes wrong. *The very inequality that these tools seek to mitigate becomes the condition that makes their risks most acute.*

There is also a troubling asymmetry at play. If a tenant uses a flawed AI-generated response in housing court, they may lose their home. If a corporate landlord uses AI to manage filings, missteps are buffered by teams of human lawyers and insurance. In a landscape where automation scales more easily for institutions than for individuals, *the benefits of legal tech risk reinforcing the very disparities they were meant to disrupt.*

That said, dismissing DoNotPay entirely would be a mistake. The ambition behind it—lowering barriers to justice through automation—is not only commendable but necessary. There is enormous potential in systems that can help users draft basic letters, understand their rights, or fill out forms accurately. Many legal processes are needlessly convoluted, and technology can serve as a bridge between people and remedies. *But the ethical deployment of such tools requires humility, transparency, and limits.*

One path forward is regulation that acknowledges nuance. Not all AI legal services are created equal. Some may provide clearly defined informational support, such as directing users to public statutes or explaining procedural steps. Others venture into personalised, context-sensitive guidance—territory that approaches or crosses the line into formal representation. *Regulatory frameworks must evolve to distinguish between these modes of engagement and to enforce standards accordingly.* Certification schemes, disclosure requirements, and mandatory human oversight for high-risk functions are possible mechanisms.

Moreover, transparency must become a core design principle. Users should know when they are interacting with a machine, what its limitations are, and what risks they face. Vague disclaimers buried in terms of use are not sufficient. Informed consent in legal technology demands more than just a checkbox; it requires *meaningful understanding*. A tool that offers to help you sue your landlord should not obscure the fact that it cannot represent you, cannot be cross-examined, and cannot correct its own logic if it misfires.

The DoNotPay case also challenges the legal profession to examine its own blind spots. If people are turning to AI chatbots for legal help, it is not merely because they are misinformed—it is because human legal services have priced themselves out of reach for too many. The profession cannot respond to AI with mere protectionism. It must offer viable alternatives: more accessible pro bono networks, simplified procedures, better public legal education, and innovative, *ethically governed* uses of technology.

At its best, DoNotPay represents a disruptive provocation—a call to reimagine how advocacy can be delivered in an age of computational power. At its worst, it represents an abdication of professional responsibility, outsourcing sensitive legal work to systems that lack the ability to reason, empathise, or be held accountable. The challenge is not to stop innovation, but to shape it in ways that respect the dignity of those it aims to serve.

The automation of advocacy is not hypothetical. It is happening. And it raises the deepest of legal questions: not only *what* law is, but *who* speaks it, *who* enforces it, and *who* takes responsibility when it goes wrong. In the age of DoNotPay, these are no longer theoretical concerns. They are live problems, encoded in algorithms, marketed in apps, and borne by real people in real legal jeopardy. What's at stake is not simply whether a robot can draft a demand letter—but whether the core values of justice, accountability, and human judgement can survive being rendered into code.

What Counts as Legal Representation?

In 2023, a man in the United States filed for asylum using an online chatbot that offered help with legal paperwork. The system walked him through a series of prompts, filled out the necessary forms, and advised him to submit the documents to immigration authorities. Only months later did he discover that the forms were outdated, the grounds of his application mischaracterised, and the advice inadmissible. By then, his claim was denied. He had no lawyer to hold accountable, no authority to appeal to, and no meaningful way to challenge the defective support he had received. The bot, after all, was not legally representing him. Or was it?

This quiet but telling incident captures the profound ambiguity at the heart of a legal system now grappling with the boundaries between guidance, representation, and automation. As artificial intelligence expands into tasks once reserved for lawyers—drafting contracts, filing disputes, answering legal questions—the line between assistance and advocacy is becoming increasingly blurred. At stake is more than professional jurisdiction. The real question is this: *what does it mean to be represented in law, and who—or what—has the right to do it?*

Traditionally, legal representation has been defined not by the tools used but by the relationship formed. A solicitor or barrister does not merely complete paperwork on a client's behalf; they owe a fiduciary duty, provide independent judgment, and are bound by professional codes. They can be disbarred, sued for malpractice, held in contempt of court. Their authority is earned, not presumed. Yet in the digital marketplace of legal services, many platforms now perform near-identical functions without those responsibilities. They parse statutes, suggest defences, auto-generate pleadings, and simulate expert reasoning—all while disclaiming any actual representation. *The service walks like a lawyer, talks like a lawyer, but denies being one at all.*

This strategic ambiguity serves both commercial and legal interests. By insisting they do not offer legal advice, many companies avoid the stringent regulations imposed on qualified professionals. They are free to operate without oversight from bar associations, free from continuing education requirements, conflict checks, or even ethical obligations. Users, meanwhile, are led to believe they're receiving expert support, unaware that such services often lack jurisdictional nuance, contingency awareness, or recourse in the event of harm. *What results is a legal grey zone where the appearance of representation conceals its absence.*

Consider the case of chatbots embedded within consumer-facing apps—tax preparation tools, landlord-tenant mediation services, or online dispute resolution platforms. Many of these systems do more than provide static information; they adapt to user input, recommend next steps, and generate documents tailored to a person's unique context. Yet when challenged, their creators often claim the outputs are "general information," not "legal advice." This distinction is crucial—and increasingly difficult to defend. If a system interprets your circumstances, applies legal norms, and offers a prescriptive course of action, *is it not, in functional terms, giving legal counsel?*

The problem is compounded by how people experience these systems. The law may draw sharp distinctions between information and advice, representation and assistance, but users do not. To them, a service that solves their legal problem feels like a lawyer. And when the system fails—due to outdated data, jurisdictional errors, or flawed logic—the fallout is not abstract. It is real: lost housing, denied asylum, missed deadlines, unenforceable claims. The consequences are borne by the user alone, while the service walks away unscathed. *A right without remedy, framed as empowerment, becomes a structural betrayal.*

Part of the difficulty lies in the current regulatory frameworks, which were built around human professionals and have not kept pace with digital practice. Most definitions of legal representation focus on intent and relationship—was there an agreement to act on someone's behalf? Was a fiduciary duty formed? These tests, while sensible in traditional contexts, falter in the face of algorithmic systems that operate at scale, across borders, and without identifiable actors. Who bears responsibility when an AI tool leads a litigant astray? The platform? The developer? The user who clicked "I accept"? *When representation is coded into software, accountability is often coded out.*

There are also jurisdictional inconsistencies. In the United States, the unauthorised practice of law (UPL) is a criminal offence in many states, but the enforcement is patchy and inconsistently interpreted. Some jurisdictions treat document automation as UPL; others allow it with disclaimers. In the UK, the approach is more permissive but equally fragmented. Legal services can be "reserved" or "unreserved," depending on the task—appearing in court requires a qualified solicitor or barrister, but giving legal advice does not necessarily demand regulation. *This mosaic of rules creates opportunities for platform creators—and confusion for everyone else.*

More than a legal issue, this is a question of public trust. The legitimacy of the justice system rests on more than procedural correctness. It depends on the belief that legal representation carries integrity, rigour, and accountability. When users cannot distinguish between a bot and a barrister, between automation and advocacy, *that trust erodes.* People begin to suspect that access to law is a game of interfaces—not of rights. And if a machine can speak the law without responsibility, *what becomes of the human institutions meant to uphold it?*

This is not to argue for a wholesale rejection of AI in legal services. On the contrary, there is immense value in responsible automation. Document automation, triage systems, legal Q&A tools, and guided workflows can enhance access, reduce delay, and unburden overstretched courts. The key, however, is transparency, scope limitation, and human fallback. Users must know when they are receiving machine-generated support. They must be told what the system can and cannot do. And they must have the option of human review where risk is high. *Representation without responsibility is not progress—it is a shell game.*

There is, then, a need for a clearer standard: one that goes beyond the binary of "lawyer" or "not lawyer," and instead focuses on the *function* being performed. When a system provides personalised legal advice, prepares documents for submission, or interprets a user's case under the law, it should be subject to similar duties as human professionals. Whether those duties are met by supervised practice, platform regulation, or professional partnerships is a policy choice. But the principle must be firm: *if it acts like representation, it must be held to the standard of representation.*

Professional bodies have a role to play—but so do technologists. Developers of legal AI must embrace a civic responsibility that extends beyond functionality. This includes designing for explainability, flagging ambiguous outcomes, integrating opt-outs, and building tools that assist rather than impersonate. Law is not simply a domain of knowledge; it is a practice of care, reasoned judgment, and ethical commitment. Any technology that wishes to operate in its space must reflect that ethos.

To ask *what counts as legal representation* in the age of AI is not merely to interrogate the legitimacy of tools—it is to revisit the purpose of representation itself. Is it about technical competence? Procedural compliance? Advocacy with empathy? Strategic discretion? The more we automate legal functions, the more we must reclarify what the human in the loop is there to do—and what the human is for. That conversation is no longer optional. It is urgent.

The threshold for representation cannot be a matter of semantics or design tricks. It must be rooted in substance: *does the service understand the user's context? Does it interpret the law? Does it make decisions or recommendations with legal consequences?* If yes, then representation—however digital or decentralised—has occurred. And it must be governed accordingly.

The rule of law is not merely a set of outputs. It is a relationship: between citizens and the institutions that speak on their behalf. That relationship demands care, clarity, and accountability. In the AI age, recognising when that relationship has been formed—and who or what has assumed the mantle of the advocate—may be one of the most important legal questions of our time.

Chapter 5
Justice at Scale

A courtroom is not a factory floor. Yet increasingly, the discourse surrounding legal technology borrows the language of logistics: throughput, optimisation, acceleration. On the surface, these terms promise a kind of salvation—a method to streamline systems weighed down by backlog, budgetary limits, and procedural inertia. But beneath the veneer of efficiency lies a more troubling question: what happens to justice when its delivery is treated as a matter of volume and velocity? This chapter begins with that tension. It is not a rejection of efficiency per se, but a sober examination of its costs.

AI-driven adjudication tools, predictive analytics, and automated triage systems now promise to process disputes more quickly, at lower cost, and on a scale previously unimaginable. For courts stretched to breaking point and administrative agencies burdened with mountains of cases, the appeal is obvious. Machines can sort tens of thousands of files in the time it takes a judge to examine a single dossier. Immigration tribunals can prioritise asylum claims. Benefits offices can detect patterns of fraud algorithmically. Civil courts can deploy risk scores to suggest early settlements. The rationale seems simple: let machines manage the predictable, leaving humans free to focus on the unpredictable.

Yet this ostensibly practical approach masks a structural inversion. In the pursuit of speed and efficiency, we risk creating systems that are no longer fundamentally designed for people. Mass adjudication tools reduce individuals to datasets, replacing context with categories and particularity with probability. The outcome is more than automation; it is depersonalisation. When the person is abstracted into a number, what remains of justice as an encounter between citizen and state?

At the heart of this tension lies a conceptual mismatch. Law, at its best, is a deliberative practice grounded in dialogue, interpretation, and moral judgment. Technology, at its most efficient, is a system of classification and execution. One asks, "What is fair here?" The other asks, "What does prior data suggest will happen?" The distinction may seem subtle, but it is foundational. A judge listens to the singularities of a defendant's story. A machine identifies the patterns that make the case typical. That difference strikes at the essence of what a legal decision is.

Consider the rise of litigation analytics: tools that mine court data to forecast the probability of success, estimate trial length, or evaluate a judge's tendencies. These systems do more than describe; they shape behaviour, deter marginal claims, and nudge parties toward early settlements. The promise is rationality and cost-effectiveness. Yet the effect is also to entrench disadvantage. If algorithms recommend avoiding cases that "score" poorly, who will champion the unconventional or morally urgent claims that defy existing patterns? In such a framework, efficiency becomes a gatekeeper rather than a gateway.

The stakes are not hypothetical. Take Australia's "Robodebt" programme: automated data matching identified alleged welfare overpayments, issuing tens of thousands of demand letters without human review. Decisions often relied on flawed or incomplete data, disproportionately affecting the most vulnerable—those with disabilities, unstable housing, or mental health challenges. The system was ultimately ruled unlawful, yet for many, the damage was irreversible. Automation did not merely fail; it obliterated the opportunity for the state to recognise and respond to individual circumstances.

What links these cases is not malice but a fundamental dissonance between the metrics of computation and the imperatives of justice. Speed is measurable. Consistency is measurable. Fairness is not. In the drive to quantify, proxies emerge: risk scores, predictive weights, algorithmic thresholds. Yet law often concerns itself with grappling, not eliminating, uncertainty. Just outcomes may be slow, inefficient, or contrary to statistical expectation—but they remain just because they engage with the unquantifiable human dimension.

Questioning justice at scale is not a call to romanticise inefficiency. Many courts are shamefully inaccessible, and digitisation can offer meaningful improvements. Yet the promise of more claims processed per hour cannot be conflated with the promise of justice.

Due process is not a set of metrics; it is a conversation. Replace that conversation with forms, flags, or scores, and the state acts without listening.

We are also witnessing a subtle reconfiguration of power. Predictive tools confer influence: a litigant warned of a 90% chance of failure may abandon a meritorious claim, even if the prediction is flawed. Agencies can justify policies on opaque data trends. Judges may defer to "neutral" algorithmic advice under mounting caseloads. When decisions are shaped by unchallengeable systems, is the rule of law functioning—or merely simulated?

The implications extend to adversarial justice itself. Prioritising cost and speed risks sidelining juries, discouraging trials, and funneling disputes into algorithmically engineered settlements. Discretion is ceded to models trained on past patterns, which carry historical biases and structural inequities. The features that make law flexible—context, compassion, and ambiguity—are reframed as errors to be corrected. Remove them, and justice becomes mechanical sorting rather than ethical engagement.

This chapter interrogates these shifts, examining the philosophical stakes of viewing law as logistics, the practical consequences of automating discretion, and the democratic risks of adjudication without accountability. It asks what it means to be truly heard, not merely processed; to be recognised as a person, not a datapoint. It challenges readers to consider whether justice delivered at scale can still be considered justice.

The question is not whether technology belongs in law; it already does. The question is whether our institutions are being reshaped in the image of technology, without adequate attention to what is lost in translation. Not all values scale. Not all truths are predictable. Not all harms can be repaired by the systems that caused them.

Justice at scale is among the defining challenges of our age. It calls for a renewed engagement with old principles—fair hearing, due process, equality before the law—with pressing urgency. We must design systems that serve not just more people, but serve them justly. Because when law moves faster than understanding, it stops being law. It becomes administration by algorithm: power without presence, resolution without redress. This chapter is an invitation to resist that drift—by asking harder questions and refusing easy answers.

Efficiency vs. Fairness

The promise that artificial intelligence will democratise justice by slashing costs and clearing case backlogs is now a familiar refrain in policy briefs, tech manifestos, and judicial reform panels. From streamlined small-claims portals to algorithmic triage systems in immigration courts, efficiency has become the watchword of legal innovation. At first glance, the rationale is difficult to challenge. In jurisdictions where justice has long been rationed by wealth, time, and geography, faster and cheaper processes seem both desirable and overdue. But beneath the appeal of accessibility lies a harder truth: *every gain in efficiency comes with a cost in discretion, detail, and deliberation.* The central question is not whether AI can help the legal system operate faster. It's whether we can afford what gets lost when it does.

Justice, unlike shipping or payroll, is not fundamentally a process of logistics. It is a normative undertaking—an exercise in judgment that weighs facts, motives, consequences, and ethical standards, case by case. When we speak of fairness, we refer not to uniformity, but to *appropriateness*: decisions that reflect the particular circumstances of individuals. Efficiency, by contrast, rewards regularity. The more standardised a process becomes, the more it can be optimised. *This is where the tension emerges: fairness thrives on exceptions; efficiency depends on their elimination.*

One need only examine the design of modern AI-powered legal systems to see this dynamic at work. Consider online dispute resolution (ODR) platforms now widely adopted in consumer, tenancy, and family law contexts. These systems guide users through pre-coded decision trees, offering step-by-step guidance based on standardised templates. They serve millions at a fraction of the cost of traditional legal advice. For routine matters—overdue rent, product refunds, uncontested divorce—they perform well. But what happens when the dispute involves family violence, cognitive disability, or cultural misunderstanding? *The platform cannot deviate from the tree. It cannot ask a question it was not programmed to consider.*

Advocates of automation argue that such limitations are acceptable trade-offs. A system that serves 90% of cases efficiently, they contend, is better than one that leaves 90% waiting. But this logic privileges procedural throughput over substantive justice. *What if the 10% left behind are those who most need the law's protection?* Worse still, the very efficiency of automated systems can mask their blind spots. Users assume the process is legitimate because it is official, accessible, and swift. Yet they may be unaware that the path they are navigating excludes critical dimensions of their experience.

This is particularly acute in areas like immigration law, where AI is increasingly deployed to assist in asylum adjudication, visa eligibility, and fraud detection. These systems often rely on natural language processing tools trained on historical case data to evaluate narrative credibility or detect inconsistency. In practice, this means that non-linear storytelling, emotional distress, or lack of documentation—common among refugees fleeing trauma—can be interpreted as red flags. The result is a cruel irony: *the more a story reflects real human suffering, the less likely it is to align with algorithmic expectations of plausibility.*

Efficiency also reshapes the behaviours of legal actors themselves. Judges under pressure to clear dockets may rely more heavily on algorithmic bail recommendations or sentencing scores. Legal aid providers may triage clients based on data-driven assessments of case viability. Even litigants, informed by litigation analytics, may choose not to pursue a claim that "scores" poorly—even when morally or legally justified. The common denominator here is risk aversion: AI tools reduce uncertainty by predicting outcomes, and those predictions in turn shape human decisions. But *when predictive systems guide legal choices, justice begins to orbit around probability rather than principle.*

Take, for example, the use of risk assessment algorithms in pre-trial detention. These tools calculate the likelihood that a defendant will reoffend or fail to appear in court, assigning them a risk score based on variables like age, prior arrests, and zip code. The goal is to reduce jail populations by identifying low-risk defendants who can be safely released. In theory, this is both efficient and equitable. In practice, it reinforces systemic biases. Factors like residential location correlate with race and poverty, not with individual dangerousness. *A system optimised for speed and general risk will inevitably make crude assumptions about people it cannot see in full.*

Proponents of AI-driven reform argue that these tools can be audited and improved—that transparency and oversight can correct for bias. And indeed, greater openness in algorithmic design is essential. But such fixes do not resolve the deeper problem: *when fairness becomes a technical calibration rather than a human deliberation, its meaning shifts.* The standard becomes: does the system treat similar inputs similarly? That may satisfy statistical parity. But it does not answer the more searching question: does this outcome respect the dignity, rights, and needs of this person?

It is worth remembering that the cost of human deliberation—the slowness, the messiness, the open-endedness—is not incidental to justice. It is intrinsic. Courts ask for testimony not because every fact can be verified, but because *the act of being heard matters.* Legal systems offer appeals not because they expect frequent reversals, but because *error must be corrigible.* These are not inefficiencies. They are commitments to a vision of justice in which people are not just variables in a function, but subjects of moral and legal concern.

The economic argument for efficiency remains strong. Legal budgets are constrained. Demand outpaces supply. Many people currently go without any legal help at all. But if access is broadened only by flattening process—by replacing depth with volume—we risk a pyrrhic victory. An automated system that resolves a complaint in minutes may appear more accessible. But if its internal logic cannot comprehend the user's real issue, what has been achieved? *Justice denied quickly is no better than justice denied slowly.*

There is another dimension to this discussion: trust. Legal legitimacy depends not just on results, but on perception. People must believe that the process is fair, even if the outcome is not in their favour. This belief is fragile. When decisions are made by machines, especially opaque ones, that trust is harder to sustain. Citizens may begin to see the law not as a forum for redress, but as an automated barrier. *A system that prioritises efficiency over empathy is not just less fair—it risks being seen as fundamentally alien.*

To navigate this dilemma, legal reformers must move beyond the binary of efficiency *versus* fairness. The task is not to reject technological assistance, but to insist that *it serve human ends without erasing human judgment.* That may mean accepting slower timelines for complex cases, investing in hybrid systems that pair automation with human review, or reimagining metrics of success to include qualitative outcomes. Above all, it means recognising that fairness is not an incidental by-product of justice—it is its foundation.

AI can and should assist in making legal systems more navigable, less expensive, and more consistent. But the aspiration must remain human: *to understand, to reason, to respond.* Without that, efficiency becomes its own justification. And justice, once streamlined past recognition, becomes something else entirely—quicker, yes, but also hollower.

In the end, the value of a legal system cannot be measured solely by its throughput, its uptime, or its cost per case. It must also be measured by its capacity to listen, to discern, and to honour the irreducible complexity of human lives. That is not an efficiency problem. That is a moral imperative. And it is one that no algorithm, however advanced, can resolve on our behalf.

The Quantified Courtroom

In the modern courtroom, numbers are beginning to speak with increasing authority. Legal forecasting tools powered by artificial intelligence now promise to predict the likelihood of winning a case, estimate settlement values, or quantify litigation risk before a single motion is filed. For law firms, insurers, and even judges, this data-driven edge holds obvious appeal. Time, cost, and uncertainty have long defined legal conflict; predictive analytics suggest these burdens can be mitigated, if not overcome. Yet what appears to be a tool of strategic clarity is also a force of epistemic shift—one that reframes how disputes are understood, evaluated, and ultimately resolved. *When outcomes are forecast in probabilities and visualised as risk curves, what becomes of persuasion, narrative, and moral judgment?* And more urgently: what becomes of the trial?

The rise of legal analytics platforms such as Lex Machina, Premonition, and Gavelytics illustrates the trend toward courtroom quantification. Drawing on decades of case law, court records, judge rulings, and party filings, these systems construct statistical profiles of litigation patterns. They might reveal, for example, that Judge X grants summary judgment motions in employment cases 78% of the time, or that plaintiffs represented by Firm Y settle medical malpractice suits 23% faster than the regional average. *Such metrics, once confined to intuition or experience, are now computable—codified into dashboards that reframe litigation as a game of informed bets.*

The implications are profound. In negotiation, data about similar cases creates powerful anchoring effects. A party advised that their claim has a 68% likelihood of success may be inclined to accept a pre-trial settlement that reflects that probability—even if they believe morally and factually in the strength of their position. For insurers and institutional defendants, this forecasting is a form of triage: high-risk cases get early attention; low-risk ones may be quietly buried or fast-tracked for dismissal. Plaintiffs' firms, meanwhile, can use analytics to vet potential clients, refusing those deemed statistically weak. *This is not the adjudication of justice in the classical sense—it is actuarial logic applied to human conflict.*

Yet there is a deeper tension at play. Predictive tools are not passive observers of the legal system—they shape the behaviour of those within it. If litigation becomes a numbers game, the incentives to craft persuasive legal argument may shrink. Lawyers may rely less on compelling facts and more on probabilistic leverage. Judges, aware that their own ruling patterns are being tracked and ranked, may become more rigid or defensive in their reasoning. And clients, conditioned by the analytics, may interpret their case not through its story, but through its score. *The quantified courtroom begins to recode legal imagination itself.*

The impact on jury trials is especially troubling. Jury trials have always been inherently unpredictable—this is, paradoxically, one of their virtues. They introduce moral deliberation into legal decision-making, allowing community values to shape outcomes in ways that written statutes or precedent might not predict. But in a system driven by risk aversion and efficiency, unpredictability is viewed not as a safeguard but as a flaw. If analytics suggest a trial is statistically disadvantageous, most rational actors will avoid it. *The result: fewer jury trials, fewer opportunities for democratic voice in adjudication, and more reliance on algorithmically informed settlement.*

There is also an asymmetry of power encoded in these systems. Large firms and government entities can afford access to premium analytics platforms, benefiting from insights unavailable to ordinary litigants or under-resourced counsel. This creates a new digital divide—*not one of connectivity, but of epistemic privilege.* One side knows how a judge has ruled in 75 similar motions; the other does not. One side can run simulations to test settlement scenarios; the other relies on guesswork. Far from levelling the playing field, courtroom quantification may entrench advantage in more opaque ways.

Proponents of these tools argue they merely make visible what experienced litigators already know: that some judges are more favourable to certain arguments, that some claims settle quickly, that some firms win more often. But codifying these tendencies into statistical certainties reifies them. *A judge with a track record of harsh sentencing may not wish to be predictable—but if data makes that pattern publicly known, they may lean into it, or struggle to escape it.* Similarly, plaintiffs may self-censor if they believe their demographic profile or jurisdictional context makes them statistically less likely to win.

This quantification extends even to individual behaviours. In criminal justice systems, risk-scoring tools such as COMPAS (Correctional Offender Management Profiling for Alternative Sanctions) assign recidivism scores to defendants based on variables like age, employment history, and past arrests. These scores can influence sentencing and parole decisions. While not strictly predictive analytics for litigation, they illustrate the same core mechanism: human futures converted into probabilities by systems opaque in logic and inflexible in judgment. Critics have noted that such tools often encode racial and economic bias, despite appearing neutral. *The more we quantify justice, the more we risk automating its existing inequalities.*

But the danger is not simply bias—it is abstraction. When a claim is translated into a statistical likelihood, its human texture can disappear. A wrongful death suit, a defamation case, or a whistleblower action may become, in the language of analytics, "an 18-month case with a 35% chance of plaintiff success and an expected damages range of $250k–400k." That description is not false—but it is hollow. *What is the price of reducing legal conflict to metadata and margins of error?*

There is also the matter of feedback loops. If legal actors increasingly rely on predictive systems to make decisions—about whether to sue, settle, or proceed to trial—the underlying data that feeds the systems becomes less diverse. Fewer outlier cases are litigated. Fewer novel arguments are tested. The model learns only from what has worked in the past. *Legal evolution, which depends on challenge and reinterpretation, becomes stunted by the very efficiency that analytics were designed to deliver.*

To be clear, there are responsible, circumspect uses of legal forecasting. When used as one input among many—alongside client values, legal merits, and moral priorities—analytics can support more informed strategy. But the line between support and substitution is thin. When the score becomes the decision, not the guide, something essential is lost. Lawyers must ask not just what the model predicts, but whether the outcome it predicts is just—and whether pursuing it aligns with the ethical obligations of counsel. *A good lawyer does not merely win; they uphold the integrity of the process.*

Indeed, this is where pedagogy becomes critical. Law schools must teach future practitioners not only how to use analytics but how to interrogate them. What assumptions underlie the model? What data does it exclude? What forms of harm or injustice might escape its detection? *Statistical literacy must be matched with normative literacy.* If we fail to cultivate this balance, we risk training lawyers to be risk managers, not advocates.

The quantified courtroom is not an aberration. It is a reflection of broader societal trends—the desire to make uncertainty calculable, to transform judgment into data, to replace messiness with manageability. But legal systems are not factories. They are institutions of public reasoning, tasked with balancing precedent and principle, equity and order. Analytics can help clarify patterns. But *justice cannot be scored like a credit rating or a weather forecast.*

What matters now is how we integrate these tools without losing sight of what law is ultimately for. Not for the efficient resolution of disputes alone, but for the meaningful recognition of persons. Not for minimising litigation exposure, but for affirming the values of fairness, dignity, and reasoned disagreement. The quantified courtroom is here—but its future depends not on code, but on conscience.

Mass Adjudication and the Death of the Individual

At the heart of any functioning justice system lies a deceptively simple premise: each person matters. Their voice, their story, their circumstances deserve to be heard and weighed on their own terms. This ideal—however aspirational—has long animated the moral foundations of legal systems across democratic societies. Yet as artificial intelligence gains traction in the machinery of adjudication, a new operational logic is asserting itself: throughput over thoughtfulness, speed over scrutiny, uniformity over nuance. In contexts such as immigration, welfare benefits, and administrative appeals, the shift toward AI-driven mass adjudication threatens to extinguish what little remains of person-centred justice. *The individual, once the locus of legal concern, is becoming a statistical residue—processed, scored, and dispatched by systems built to manage scale, not meaning.*

Governments under pressure to reduce caseload backlogs, curb administrative costs, and expedite public service delivery have increasingly embraced automation in their adjudicative functions. Nowhere is this more visible than in immigration systems. In the United States, the Department of Homeland Security has trialled AI-assisted triage tools to sort visa applications by perceived risk; in Canada, the Immigration and Refugee Board has used algorithmic screening to prioritise refugee claims based on nationality and historical success rates. The European Union has funded projects exploring AI deployment in asylum processing—systems designed to assist, and in some cases replace, initial human review.

The appeal is obvious. Immigration systems face chronic overload. In the UK, for instance, delays in asylum processing have left tens of thousands in limbo for months or years. Automating parts of the decision process promises to increase efficiency, reduce human error, and free up overburdened adjudicators for complex cases. But *efficiency is not the same as justice*, and the logic of mass adjudication introduces a raft of normative concerns. When decisions about status, rights, and deportation are driven by pattern-matching algorithms rather than deliberative human judgment, *what room remains for moral discernment?*

Central to the problem is the flattening of lived complexity into quantifiable inputs. Algorithmic decision systems must, by necessity, rely on structured data: checkboxes, codes, standardised responses. The narrative voice—the detailed account of persecution, trauma, or hardship—becomes secondary, or even excluded. A claimant whose story doesn't neatly align with a pre-coded template may find their case flagged as anomalous, unreliable, or lower priority. *The very human messiness that makes a case unique is treated as noise in a system trained to seek conformity.* And when AI models are trained on past outcomes, they risk replicating historic biases—embedding systemic prejudices into supposedly neutral code.

This abstraction is not confined to immigration. Welfare and benefits adjudication, long mired in bureaucratic complexity, has similarly turned to automation to expedite eligibility decisions. The Dutch government's "SyRI" system, designed to detect welfare fraud, combined data from multiple state databases to identify individuals deemed high-risk for investigation. It was ultimately struck down by the courts in 2020 for violating privacy and human rights, but not before causing real harm. In the UK, the use of AI systems to assess disability benefits and Universal Credit applications has drawn criticism for opaque decision-making and an overreliance on flawed data inputs. *In each instance, the human subject is rendered an object of analysis—reduced to a risk score, a probability, a flag on a dashboard.*

Critically, these systems often lack meaningful avenues for appeal or explanation. When decisions are automated, recipients may receive determinations without clear reasoning or the ability to interrogate the basis of the outcome. If an AI system determines that an individual is ineligible for housing support, or that their refugee claim lacks "credibility markers," what recourse do they have to challenge that judgment—especially when even the administrators may not understand the algorithm's internal logic? *Opacity becomes a structural injustice, compounding the power imbalance between state and citizen.*

This trend toward depersonalised adjudication is not accidental; it reflects a broader ideological orientation—one that frames justice not as a deliberative public good, but as a logistical challenge to be optimised. It is a vision that sees the law not as a human endeavour but as an administrative burden to be minimised through technical innovation. In this framework, *individuality is friction.* And friction, in systems designed for scale, is the enemy.

Yet friction is precisely where justice often resides. The outlier case, the story that defies precedent, the claimant whose truth doesn't fit a template—these are not exceptions to be filtered out. They are the very reason adjudication exists. Legal systems are not merely systems of rule enforcement; they are institutions of recognition. They exist to listen, to judge, to respond to human particularity. *To erase that particularity in the name of speed or cost-saving is to commit a category error—mistaking management for meaning.*

Consider the implications for vulnerable populations. Refugees fleeing persecution, disabled claimants seeking dignity, low-income families requesting housing assistance—these are not just administrative units in a database. They are people whose lives often already stand at the margins of power. When the system designed to adjudicate their needs becomes indifferent to their individuality, it reinforces the very marginalisation it purports to address. Worse, it does so under the guise of neutrality, disguising value-laden decisions as "objective" outputs of code.

Defenders of AI-driven adjudication argue that human discretion is itself flawed—subject to bias, inconsistency, and delay. They are not wrong. But replacing one flawed process with another does not guarantee improvement, especially when the new system *obscures its biases behind the veil of statistical rationality.* The real question is not whether humans or machines are better at making decisions; it is what kind of decision-making we want our legal systems to reflect.

Do we value speed above all? Or are we willing to accept messiness, complexity, and cost as the price of a justice system that sees the individual, not just the pattern?

There are, of course, hybrid models. Systems in which AI supports, but does not supplant, human adjudicators. Systems that flag inconsistencies or suggest outcomes, but leave final judgment in human hands. These are preferable in theory—but they are vulnerable in practice. Once automated tools are integrated, economic and political pressures push towards fuller automation. Decision support becomes decision delegation. *The human judge becomes the rubber stamp, not the conscience of the process.*

Reclaiming person-centred justice in an age of mass adjudication requires more than technical reform; it requires a normative reorientation. Policymakers must ask not only *can* we automate this decision, but *should* we? Developers of legal AI must embed contestability, transparency, and dignity into system design. And legal institutions must resist the lure of scale when it comes at the cost of humanity.

Ultimately, justice is not defined by how many cases we can process per hour. It is defined by whether each person who enters the system feels they have been seen, heard, and treated with respect. If we allow efficiency to override empathy, if we trade recognition for throughput, *we do not have justice at scale—we have bureaucracy at speed.* The death of the individual in adjudication is not an inevitability. It is a choice. And it is one we must have the courage to refuse.

Redefining Due Process

In any society that dares to call itself just, *due process is not a procedural nicety—it is the architecture of fairness itself.* It is the promise that before the state exercises power over a person's life, liberty, or property, there will be reasoned deliberation, meaningful participation, and impartial adjudication. Yet as artificial intelligence reshapes the administrative and judicial machinery of modern governance, this centuries-old doctrine faces an unprecedented tension: the collision between deliberative justice and computational speed. When digital systems are calibrated for velocity, scalability, and cost-efficiency, *what remains of due process when its core values become computational obstacles rather than guiding principles?*

Speed is not, in itself, the enemy of justice. Timeliness has always mattered—especially for those waiting on asylum, child custody decisions, or access to benefits. Delays can be punitive, turning procedural fairness into protracted suffering. But the danger arises when speed becomes the *defining metric* of a system's legitimacy. When faster decisions are celebrated without scrutinising their depth or legitimacy, *we begin to conflate resolution with justice*—as though the absence of delay is proof of due process fulfilled.

The advent of AI-fuelled adjudication systems has dramatically intensified this pressure. Whether in tax disputes, visa applications, parole hearings, or fraud investigations, machine-driven decision tools now operate across multiple tiers of legal and quasi-legal governance. These systems can parse thousands of cases in a fraction of the time a human tribunal would require. But they often *sacrifice the deliberative dimension that due process was designed to protect.*

Consider the deployment of "risk assessment algorithms" in bail and sentencing decisions. In the United States, software like COMPAS generates recidivism scores to help judges decide whether a defendant should be released pretrial. The logic is simple: predict future behaviour based on past patterns, and reduce subjective bias. Yet these systems often operate with proprietary algorithms, opaque inputs, and no clear mechanism for defendants to challenge their assessment. *A person may be denied liberty based on a score they cannot interrogate, generated by a system whose logic even the court cannot fully explain.* That is not due process—it is administrative convenience cloaked in digital legitimacy.

Even in systems with nominal human oversight, algorithmic triage can bias the outcome long before a judge sees the case. For example, in the UK's immigration system, automated case-routing tools help determine which applications receive expedited processing and which are delayed for "complexity." While these systems aim to streamline caseloads, they risk pre-sorting cases in ways that entrench disadvantage. If an applicant's nationality, travel history, or language proficiency are algorithmically linked to lower success rates, their file may receive less scrutiny or attention. *The initial filter, not the final hearing, becomes the locus of judgment.*

The problem is compounded when legal systems rely on AI to determine eligibility for procedural rights in the first place. In several jurisdictions, welfare claimants must pass automated assessments before qualifying for an in-person review. If the machine denies the claim and the system lacks clear mechanisms for appeal, the result is a silent miscarriage of justice: *no hearing, no voice, no review—just a closed file and a digitised rejection.*

This shift in the architecture of adjudication reveals a deeper transformation. *The idea of due process is being gradually unmoored from its philosophical foundations.* Traditionally, due process has served both a functional role (ensuring fair outcomes) and a dignitary one (affirming the individual's moral status as a subject of rights). The process was valued not just for its result, but because it *recognised the person*—inviting them to speak, to challenge, to be heard. In the computational model of adjudication, that moral recognition is increasingly displaced by data processing. The system listens only to the structured fields it knows how to parse.

Critically, this erosion of process is not always visible. When delays disappear and outcomes arrive faster, there is often a perception of improvement. But speed can be deceptive. An immigration tribunal that processes 10,000 claims in a month using automated templates may report a backlog cleared. But how many of those claimants understood the decision? How many were denied on the basis of heuristics that failed to capture the nuance of their story? *When deliberation is replaced by data-matching, the appearance of justice masks its evaporation.*

One of the foundational insights of modern legal theory is that *fairness requires the opportunity to contest.* It is not enough to receive a decision—one must be able to question the rationale behind it, to present counter-evidence, to demand explanation. Yet many AI-driven systems are built without this capacity. The logic of machine learning often precludes transparency. Developers themselves may not fully understand how neural networks arrive at specific outputs.

As such, affected parties may be subject to decisions that no human can justify—and that no institution can reverse.

This undermines not just the procedural integrity of due process, but its democratic legitimacy. Law is not a product to be consumed efficiently; it is a process that binds the governed to their governors. When decisions feel arbitrary, inscrutable, or unchallengeable, *citizens lose faith not only in outcomes but in the institutions themselves*. And when legal systems become automated black boxes, accountability disappears alongside agency. The state remains powerful, but no longer answerable.

To be clear, not all automation is incompatible with due process. Properly designed AI systems can aid transparency by standardising reasoning, flagging inconsistencies, and ensuring uniform treatment. But the key lies in *how* these tools are integrated—and *who* retains final authority. When AI supports human deliberation rather than replacing it, when systems are built with contestability and interpretability in mind, due process can be preserved—perhaps even enhanced. But this requires a radical shift in both design philosophy and institutional mindset.

Legal technologists must resist the seduction of speed for its own sake. Developers must prioritise explainability, embedding procedural safeguards into the architecture of their tools. Lawmakers must set standards for transparency, appealability, and data quality before deploying AI in decision-making contexts. And courts must remain vigilant, refusing to treat algorithmic outputs as dispositive or unchallengeable.

Most of all, we must remember what due process is *for*. It is not a bureaucratic hurdle. It is a moral stance: *that people matter, and that decisions about their lives must be made with care, reason, and respect.* If the digital transformation of law proceeds without this orientation, we may gain speed—but at the cost of losing the very soul of justice. Deliberation is not a delay to be minimised; it is the practice through which law affirms its legitimacy. *Without it, what remains is not process, but administration—and not due, but denied.*

Chapter 6
Bias In, Bias Out

The allure of artificial intelligence in law is immediate and seductive: impartial machines, free from emotion, precedent, or prejudice, making decisions purely on merit. This narrative of neutrality has become central to the marketing of algorithmic tools, which promise to enhance fairness by eliminating human error. Yet this vision rests on a fundamental misconception—that the absence of consciousness equates to the absence of bias. In reality, AI systems inherit the politics, assumptions, and blind spots of their creators. They do not transcend prejudice; they operationalise it, often more systematically, opaquely, and pervasively than any single human could.

To grasp this, one must discard the notion of AI as an external, neutral force imposed upon the legal system. Algorithms emerge from within the very institutions whose histories they claim to surpass. The datasets underpinning them—arrest records, conviction statistics, litigation outcomes—are anything but pristine reflections of reality. They are saturated with the assumptions, discretionary choices, and structural inequities of decades, sometimes centuries, of law shaped by racial and economic stratification. Feed such history into a model, and bias is not eliminated—it is codified, parameterised, and scaled.

Consider predictive policing systems, which claim to optimise the deployment of law enforcement resources based on statistical risk. Tools such as PredPol, used across numerous American cities, purport to forecast where crime will occur. In practice, they forecast where arrests have historically occurred—a markedly different proposition. Arrest data is not a neutral measure of crime; it is a record of where police have chosen to patrol. Given the long-standing concentration of policing in economically disadvantaged and minority communities, these models reflect surveillance patterns, not actual criminal incidence. The algorithms then reinforce these patterns: more officers are sent to the same areas, more arrests are made, and the data "validates" the model. This is not intelligence; it is automated confirmation bias.

Perhaps even more insidious is the veneer of scientific legitimacy such systems project. A human judge basing suspicion on a defendant's postcode would be rightly condemned as profiling. Yet when an algorithm produces a similar outcome through historical correlations, it is reframed as evidence-based reasoning. The opacity of machine learning shields bias from scrutiny, making prejudice actionable under the guise of objectivity.

Bias, however, also arises from what is absent in the data. Historical datasets frequently underrepresent marginalised communities, whose experiences were systematically ignored. Consider natural language processing models used in legal document review: they may misinterpret or flag expressions from Indigenous or immigrant communities as anomalies, simply because such linguistic forms were insufficiently represented during training. Skewed inclusion is one problem; structural absence is another, equally consequential.

Technical "fixes" often miss this structural reality. Much discussion of algorithmic bias centres on data hygiene: masking protected attributes, de-biasing inputs, applying fairness metrics post hoc. While these measures have merit, they presume bias is a contaminant, rather than an intrinsic property of the system. If the law being modelled is itself inequitable, the algorithm learns the law's inequities faithfully. Technical optimisation, in this sense, risks enshrining injustice rather than mitigating it.

The stakes are stark in sentencing and parole. COMPAS, a widely used risk assessment tool in the United States, evaluates defendants' likelihood of reoffending. Investigations revealed that the system disproportionately labelled Black defendants as high-risk while underestimating the risk for white defendants. Removing race as an input did little: proxies such as prior arrests, residential stability, or employment history encoded the same racialised biases. The machine did not internalise constitutional values; it absorbed the biases embedded in its training data.

Challenging algorithmic decisions is fraught. Legal safeguards—cross-examination, discovery, judicial review—presume transparency. Yet many AI systems are proprietary, shielded by trade secrecy, and opaque even to the courts themselves. A defendant may face a sentence influenced by a score they cannot interrogate, from a system whose reasoning is inaccessible. Accountability evaporates into intellectual property, while bias calcifies behind legal protections. Discrimination becomes not merely statistical, but procedural—a crisis of due process.

This is not merely hypothetical. The Netherlands' SyRI system, designed to detect social welfare fraud, disproportionately targeted residents of poor, immigrant-heavy neighbourhoods, sparking a national outcry and eventual court intervention. Yet for countless other systems, bias persists quietly, affecting lives without public awareness or recourse. Opacity, in this sense, is not an accidental flaw—it is a structural feature.

Crucially, bias does not require ill intent to operate. Developers often believe in the progressive potential of AI. Yet good intentions do not inoculate against bad outcomes. Technological intervention, assumed to be inherently virtuous, can replicate systemic inequities at unprecedented scale. Smarter systems can administer injustice more efficiently than ever.

This is not to argue for the abandonment of AI in law. But it does demand a profound rethinking of design, deployment, and governance. We must ask not simply whether a system is "biased," but whose values it encodes, whose histories it reflects, whose voices it ignores, and who bears responsibility for its errors. These are constitutional, not merely engineering, questions.

The myth of neutrality is not merely false; it is politically hazardous. It allows decision-makers to defer responsibility, to cede authority to opaque systems, and to recast inequality as inevitability. AI does not inherently make law fairer. Left unchecked, it makes law faster, more consistent, and more inscrutable—a dangerous combination. If bias is baked into the data, and the system relies on that data, then bias is not an aberration; it is the outcome.

This chapter proceeds from that recognition. It does not reject AI in law, but insists upon an honest, rigorous, and structural reckoning with its risks. Without such scrutiny, we risk constructing the most efficient legal system imaginable—and codifying discrimination with unprecedented precision.

The Myth of Neutrality

The idea that artificial intelligence can deliver justice free from human bias is not just optimistic—it is profoundly misinformed. The fantasy of neutrality has always been a convenient fiction in the history of institutional power, but in the domain of algorithmic decision-making, it takes on an especially dangerous form. When AI is positioned as a rational arbiter—untainted by prejudice, immune to emotion, and governed only by data—it becomes harder to interrogate, challenge, or even perceive its partialities. *The machine does not appear to discriminate; it merely calculates.* But beneath this computational calm lies a brutal truth: algorithms are not born neutral—they are trained on the world as it is, not the world as it ought to be.

Every system of artificial intelligence that purports to make decisions, from credit scoring and bail determinations to predictive policing and job screening, relies on data. But data is not a raw, objective record of reality. It is collected, cleaned, categorised, and interpreted by human beings operating within political, economic, and social frameworks. This means that datasets reflect the prejudices of the societies from which they are drawn. When we feed these patterns into AI systems, we are not eliminating bias—we are encoding it in logic, formalising it as policy, and removing it from the reach of accountability. *Bias does not disappear in an algorithm; it becomes institutionalised.*

Consider the infamous COMPAS system used in criminal justice across the United States. Designed to predict a defendant's risk of reoffending, COMPAS has been used to inform sentencing and parole decisions. Its creators claimed it offered objective insights. Yet investigations revealed that it consistently flagged Black defendants as higher risk than white defendants, even when controlling for actual rates of recidivism. The system's defenders argued that it did not use race as a variable. But this is precisely the point. *Discrimination often functions through proxies.* Factors such as prior arrests, residential instability, or employment gaps are not neutral indicators—they are deeply intertwined with race, poverty, and historical discrimination.

This problem is not confined to American courts. Across Europe, AI systems have been used to automate decisions on immigration, welfare eligibility, and fraud detection. In the Netherlands, the SyRI system combined data from multiple government agencies to flag citizens as potential welfare cheats. In practice, it disproportionately targeted residents in poor, immigrant-heavy neighbourhoods. After public outcry and legal challenges, the system was declared in violation of human rights. *The algorithm did not invent inequality—it simply inherited and amplified it.*

The allure of algorithmic objectivity often obscures the fact that every decision in building an AI system is a human choice. Which variables to include, how to weigh them, which data to train on, how to define success—all of these are ethical and political judgments masquerading as technical ones. A tool trained to predict "successful employees" may learn to privilege candidates from certain universities, who happen to be overwhelmingly white and wealthy. A chatbot trained on existing legal documents may learn to replicate outdated legal norms that disadvantage women or minorities. *There is no such thing as an apolitical model—only unacknowledged politics encoded in code.*

One might think the solution lies in simply excluding sensitive variables—race, gender, religion—from the training data. But this approach misunderstands how bias operates. Discrimination does not always require direct reference to protected categories; it often emerges through correlation. Zip codes, for example, are strongly predictive of race and income. Linguistic patterns may correlate with ethnicity or class. Health records may reflect medical racism in diagnosis and treatment. *Removing the explicit marker does not erase the implicit pattern.*

Moreover, neutrality is often defined in relation to the status quo. AI systems that aim to reproduce "successful" past outcomes—such as effective policing, efficient courts, or profitable lending—implicitly treat existing patterns as desirable. But if the historical record is marred by systemic injustice, then using it as a benchmark entrenches inequality. An algorithm that rewards loan applicants who resemble past recipients will naturally prefer those who were already advantaged. A tool that prioritises legal strategies that have won in the past may overlook novel or justice-seeking arguments. *In such systems, fairness is defined by precedent, not principle.*

The myth of neutrality also reshapes power dynamics. When a judge makes a biased ruling, there is at least a person to challenge, a logic to interrogate, a process for appeal. When an AI makes a decision, the pathway is often opaque—hidden behind proprietary code, trade secrecy, or technical complexity. This opacity creates what legal scholars call a "black box" problem: we do not know how the system arrived at its decision, and therefore cannot effectively contest it. *The appearance of objectivity deflects scrutiny, even as it denies accountability.*

These dynamics are especially troubling in contexts involving vulnerable populations. In immigration adjudication, for instance, AI tools have been proposed to assess the credibility of asylum seekers based on language analysis or behavioural cues. But such metrics are culturally biased and notoriously unreliable. They reduce complex human narratives—often shaped by trauma, translation, and fear—into quantifiable risk scores. In doing so, they erase the very individuality that justice is meant to protect. *Neutrality here becomes a mechanism of dismissal, not discernment.*

Defenders of algorithmic tools often argue that while imperfect, they are still less biased than humans. Judges, police officers, and hiring managers are undeniably fallible. But this comparison misunderstands the nature of scale and speed. Human bias, while harmful, is bounded. Algorithmic bias is systematised, instantaneous, and replicable across millions of cases. *It is the difference between flawed judgment and automated injustice.*

To address these risks, some have proposed bias audits, fairness metrics, and algorithmic impact assessments. These are important steps. But they do not solve the foundational issue: that most AI systems are designed to optimise outcomes, not interrogate values. A tool built to maximise efficiency, profit, or conviction rates may be "fair" in mathematical terms but still unjust in practice. *What we optimise reflects what we prioritise—and what we prioritise reveals who we protect.*

Neutrality, then, is not a property of machines—it is a claim made by their creators. And it is a claim that must be subjected to democratic scrutiny. Just as the legal system itself evolved through contestation, deliberation, and reform, so too must its computational extensions. We cannot outsource justice to systems we do not understand, built on histories we do not examine, with values we do not define.

If we are to use AI in the pursuit of justice, we must abandon the illusion that it will deliver neutrality. What it offers, instead, is a mirror—one that reflects our institutional memory, our normative priorities, and our collective blind spots. The question is not whether AI is biased. It is *whether we are willing to confront how our own systems have taught it to be so.*

Predictive Policing: A Case Study in Amplified Injustice

A police officer patrolling a quiet neighbourhood is directed to make routine stops not because of a recent crime, a citizen complaint, or a tip from the community, but because an algorithm predicted a likelihood of future trouble based on patterns buried in decades of data. The result is a circular feedback loop where surveillance justifies itself, presence provokes the very incidents it purports to prevent, and injustice becomes automated in the name of objectivity. At the heart of this system lies predictive policing—a set of technologies that promise foresight but too often deliver distortion, disproportionately burdening the most vulnerable and obscuring the very biases it was supposed to eliminate.

Predictive policing tools emerged with the allure of data-driven decision-making at a time when public institutions were desperate for efficiency and accountability. Promising to predict where crimes were likely to occur, who might commit them, and who was most at risk of becoming a victim, companies like PredPol (Predictive Policing) marketed their services to hundreds of police departments across the United States and beyond. The software used historical crime data—time, location, offence type—to generate patrol recommendations. Ostensibly neutral, these maps of "high-risk" areas came to dictate real-world policing strategies.

Yet beneath the surface of these tidy crime forecasts lies a far messier reality. Historical crime data is not a faithful reflection of all criminal activity; it is a record of police decisions—who they stopped, where they patrolled, which neighbourhoods they prioritised, and which infractions they chose to record. In urban centres, this often meant disproportionate surveillance of poor, Black, and Latino communities. These communities appear overrepresented in crime databases not because more crime necessarily occurs there, but because more policing occurs there. *The data is not objective—it is already a product of bias.*

When predictive systems rely on these data sets, they amplify the distortions. A neighbourhood marked as high-risk today is more heavily policed tomorrow. More arrests follow—not necessarily for more serious crimes, but often for minor infractions that would be ignored elsewhere. These arrests feed back into the system as new "crime data," reinforcing the designation of the area as high-risk. *The algorithm creates a self-fulfilling prophecy, entrenching surveillance through a veneer of scientific neutrality.*

PredPol is not alone in this pattern. COMPAS (Correctional Offender Management Profiling for Alternative Sanctions), a tool used to assess the likelihood that a defendant will reoffend, has been adopted in sentencing and bail decisions across multiple states. It claims to use dozens of variables to offer risk scores. Yet investigative journalism has shown that COMPAS tends to overpredict recidivism among Black defendants and underpredict it for white defendants. In one widely cited study by ProPublica, two defendants with similar criminal histories received sharply different risk assessments. The only discernible difference? Race.

What makes this so dangerous is the opacity. These systems are often proprietary; their methodologies are hidden under trade secrets. Judges, lawyers, and defendants cannot interrogate the models. There is no requirement for public audits, no obligation to disclose the data sets used, no standard for assessing bias. *Decisions that profoundly affect individual lives—whether someone remains in jail, how long they serve, where officers concentrate their time—are increasingly driven by tools that are shielded from scrutiny.*

Some defenders argue that predictive policing simply points officers to areas with higher reported crime, and that human judgment ultimately controls outcomes. But this defence ignores how institutional incentives evolve. Officers under pressure to justify deployments are more likely to stop and cite individuals in algorithmically "hot" zones, even for minor violations. Prosecutors and judges—overburdened by caseloads—may defer to machine-generated risk scores in bail or sentencing decisions. *The existence of a predictive system subtly reshapes the behaviours and assumptions of everyone in the legal pipeline.*

Moreover, the very idea of "crime prediction" elides deeper social dynamics. Most predictive policing systems focus on so-called street crimes—burglary, assault, drug offences—while ignoring white-collar crimes, domestic abuse, or systemic corruption. These omissions are not random. They reflect decades of policing priorities shaped by politics, race, and economic interest. In practice, predictive policing systems are less about forecasting crime and more about *reinforcing institutional focus on the criminalisation of poverty.*

International examples confirm that this is not uniquely American. In the United Kingdom, the Durham Constabulary piloted the Harm Assessment Risk Tool (HART), an algorithm used to predict the likelihood of an individual committing a serious crime. It used data from over 100 variables, including postcode and past police contact. The use of such inputs—many of which correlate strongly with socio-economic status—raised immediate ethical concerns. Even with efforts to address bias, the core issue remained: when you build systems to "score" people based on the past, you risk cementing the very inequalities you ought to mitigate.

The philosophical problem is profound. Predictive policing claims to move from reactive justice to proactive prevention. But this shift changes the moral architecture of law enforcement. Instead of investigating crimes and upholding rights, policing becomes a speculative enterprise—treating individuals and communities as future risks to be managed rather than present citizens to be served. *It transforms the presumption of innocence into a probability of guilt.*

Efforts to reform predictive policing often focus on technical solutions: better data hygiene, more inclusive training sets, fairness-aware machine learning. These are valuable but limited. They address symptoms, not the source. If the problem is that the data reflects structural injustice, then improving the data does not solve the underlying inequities—it merely updates them. If the model is optimised for police efficiency, it will continue to reward aggressive enforcement even if it becomes statistically fairer. *Fairness metrics do not replace political judgment; they can only complement it.*

More fundamentally, predictive policing shifts the locus of accountability. When discriminatory patterns emerge, it becomes easier for institutions to blame the algorithm. "The system made the call" becomes a shield against responsibility. Yet the algorithm is not a rogue actor—it is an institutional artefact, shaped by designers, coders, administrators, and decision-makers. *Responsibility diffused through code is still responsibility.*

Perhaps the most disturbing feature of predictive policing is that it works *just well enough* to justify its own use. When departments say that predictive tools "help allocate resources" or "reduce response times," they are often reporting on metrics defined by the same systems they deployed. A reduction in recorded crime may reflect changed police practices, not actual safety. Success becomes a circular narrative: the tool is effective because it said it would be, and because its users believe it is. *This is not empirical validation; it is institutional reinforcement.*

To grapple honestly with predictive policing requires more than tweaks to code or data. It demands a reckoning with how we define safety, how we build trust, and whose lives are deemed worthy of dignity rather than suspicion. The promise of AI is often framed in terms of efficiency—but justice is not merely a matter of speed or accuracy. It is a matter of values, of visibility, of treating people as more than statistical risks.

A just society must decide whether it is willing to accept statistical discrimination in the name of predictive power, or whether it values the human complexities that defy easy classification. Predictive policing, as it currently operates, invites us to believe that data can see the future. But if we are not vigilant, it may only teach us to repeat the past—with greater speed, greater certainty, and less accountability. And that is not progress. It is algorithmic injustice in its most refined form.

Bias by Omission: How Excluded Populations Distort the Architecture of Legal AI

An algorithm trained to recommend bail decisions performs well—on paper. It processes tens of thousands of historical court records, learns from statistical correlations, and produces recommendations with high consistency. But what if those court records omitted a key population: undocumented immigrants, transgender individuals, or victims of domestic abuse who never reported their cases? What if the algorithm learned from a legal landscape that never fully accounted for certain lives? The result is not merely an incomplete picture. It is a *distorted* one. *Bias by omission is not a gap in data—it is a structural absence that deforms the frame through which justice is calculated.*

Legal AI systems increasingly rely on large-scale datasets to automate tasks traditionally performed by human experts: risk assessments, sentencing recommendations, contract analysis, and even judicial reasoning. These systems are often described as impartial, capable of standardising outcomes, reducing backlogs, and improving access. But the neutrality of the output depends entirely on the completeness of the input. When datasets reflect only certain experiences, or exclude others entirely, the legal conclusions they enable are not just imprecise—they become inequitable in ways that are difficult to detect, let alone correct.

Consider predictive risk scoring tools used in child welfare systems, such as those trialled in Allegheny County, Pennsylvania. The algorithm assesses the likelihood of a child suffering harm based on historical data: parental arrest records, public benefit usage, housing instability. On the surface, it appears rigorous. Yet these data points are far more available for low-income families who interact frequently with government systems. Middle-class families, especially those using private services, are underrepresented. The system thus becomes *more confident in assessing the poor*, not because they are at greater inherent risk, but because they are more visible in the dataset. *Omission, in this case, does not mean silence—it means the amplification of one experience over another, codified into policy.*

A similar pattern emerges in immigration adjudication. When machine learning is used to model refugee outcomes or asylum decisions, it is typically trained on years of case law. But these cases represent those who made it into the system—who filed, who testified, who were recorded. The thousands who never applied, who were deterred, who disappeared, are absent. An AI trained on such a record will learn patterns of success based on what is *visible*, not what is structurally absent. It may overvalue certain legal arguments or downplay others, not because those strategies are ineffective, but because they were never tried. The data becomes a hall of mirrors—self-referential, bounded, and circular.

Omissions are not random. They are the result of historical inequalities that dictated who was counted, who was documented, who had access to representation. In medical AI, it is now widely acknowledged that many early models performed poorly on darker skin tones because training datasets overrepresented light-skinned patients. In legal AI, the equivalent phenomenon is subtler but no less dangerous. A contract review tool that flags "risky" clauses based on past litigation outcomes may fail to identify exploitative language that has simply never been challenged in court—often because the affected party lacked resources, knowledge, or legal standing. *The algorithm doesn't see injustice that was never formally recorded as such.*

And when omission becomes systemic, it produces *epistemic injustice*—a condition in which some individuals or communities are not merely misrepresented, but rendered illegible within the knowledge structures that shape policy and law. Legal interpretation becomes skewed not by malice, but by invisibility. The people most vulnerable to harm are often the least legible to the systems designed to protect them. This is not a technical flaw; it is a moral crisis.

Attempts to mitigate bias by omission often focus on expanding training datasets: collecting more cases, sourcing from more jurisdictions, including diverse populations. This is necessary, but not sufficient. The problem is not only quantity, but *structure*. If the historical record reflects centuries of racialised policing, gendered violence, or socio-economic stratification, then simply scaling the dataset may entrench those same biases at higher resolution. Bigger data does not mean better justice. It may just mean *more detailed discrimination.*

Legal technologists sometimes propose synthetic data—artificially generated cases that simulate underrepresented experiences—as a workaround. But this raises complex ethical questions: who decides what a "typical" undocumented worker's case looks like? How do we avoid injecting new stereotypes in the name of balance? Without grounding in lived experience, synthetic corrections risk becoming speculative fictions that further disconnect systems from reality.

Another response is the push for explainable AI (XAI), which seeks to clarify how algorithms arrive at decisions. Transparency helps—but it does not resolve omission. One can perfectly explain a decision made from biased data. A transparent injustice is still an injustice. What is needed is not just technical interpretability, but a normative conversation about *which voices get encoded into law*.

This calls for a rethinking of what constitutes "data" in legal contexts. Testimonies from marginalised communities, oral histories, qualitative research, community reports—these are often excluded from formal datasets because they are not easily quantifiable. Yet they contain the very knowledge that could help correct skewed interpretations. Legal AI must evolve from mere data science into a discipline that honours *epistemic pluralism*—valuing multiple forms of knowing, even when they resist statistical formalisation.

The stakes are highest where automated decisions replace human discretion. In the United Kingdom, automation was introduced to process certain welfare benefits, including Universal Credit claims. Claimants were required to interface with digital systems that used rules-based logic and historical norms to assess eligibility. But the system frequently failed to recognise non-standard life situations—freelancers, carers, refugees—because the datasets used to model "typical" claimants had excluded them. As a result, *nonconformity became risk*. Those who didn't fit the mould were not just inconvenienced—they were penalised, delayed, or denied. The algorithmic system interpreted deviation not as complexity, but as fraud.

The deeper philosophical question is this: *Can a system of justice built on incomplete data ever be legitimate?* Traditional legal reasoning, for all its flaws, has long recognised the importance of interpretation, narrative, and judgment. Judges weigh evidence not only based on frequency, but on credibility and context. They listen to stories. Algorithms, by contrast, flatten stories into features and weights. When the data is partial, the story is partial. And when the story is partial, justice becomes a statistical hallucination.

The danger of omission is especially insidious because it masquerades as neutrality. While biased inputs or discriminatory outputs can be debated and often detected, omissions are harder to trace. Their effects accumulate silently: a slightly lower risk score here, a denied claim there, an overlooked precedent that subtly shifts jurisprudence. Over time, these minor exclusions become macro-injustices—normalised and invisible.

A more just future demands that we confront this invisibility head-on. Not only by adding missing data, but by interrogating *why* it was missing to begin with. Whose experiences were excluded, and by whose design? What assumptions shaped the data collection? What institutional blind spots were baked into the archival process? *These are not questions that algorithms can answer. They require human reflection, humility, and historical awareness.*

Bias by omission is not a bug—it is a mirror. It reflects back the selective memory of our legal institutions, the uneven terrain of our civic records, and the structural exclusions we have yet to redress. If we are to build AI that genuinely enhances justice rather than mechanising inequality, we must begin not with the machine, but with a clearer understanding of the world it fails to see. Only then can we hope to build systems that do not merely replicate our past, but reckon with it.

Fixing the Inputs Isn't Enough: Why Clean Data Can't Undo Dirty Histories

In 2016, a high-profile study revealed that COMPAS, a risk assessment tool used across the United States to inform bail and sentencing decisions, disproportionately flagged Black defendants as high risk of reoffending—despite having similar recidivism rates to white defendants. The outcry that followed generated a wave of responses: some dismissed the tool as flawed, others defended its statistical accuracy, and many offered a familiar prescription—*clean the data.* The assumption was seductive: better inputs would yield fairer outputs. But this is a dangerous illusion. *Bias in AI is not merely a technical problem of data cleanliness; it is a structural feature of the social and legal systems in which these tools operate.*

To treat bias as a contamination in the dataset is to misunderstand its origin. Bias in legal technology is not a bug in the code or a smudge on the spreadsheet. It is the digital crystallisation of decades—often centuries—of policies, decisions, and omissions that shape who gets arrested, who gets prosecuted, who gets silenced, and who gets believed. Cleaning the inputs without confronting that history is like scrubbing the surface of a shattered mirror. The reflection may look sharper, but the image remains fractured.

In criminal justice, for instance, arrest data is often used to train AI models that forecast future crime or recidivism. But arrest data reflects not just crime rates, but *enforcement patterns*: where police choose to patrol, which communities they surveil, how officers exercise discretion. It encodes practices influenced by race, class, geography, and politics. Efforts to "clean" such datasets typically involve removing obvious outliers, standardising formats, or balancing demographic variables. Yet none of these interventions challenge the deeper fact that the dataset itself is *a product of biased institutional behaviour.*

The problem worsens when these datasets are deployed under the guise of objectivity. The myth of neutral computation allows policymakers to defer to machine outputs, confident that the system is now "fair" because the inputs have been sanitised. But fairness cannot be retrofitted through statistical trickery. An algorithm trained on decades of redlining, selective prosecution, or economic exclusion does not shed those ghosts simply because we've anonymised the data or balanced the categories. *There is no checkbox in a spreadsheet for structural injustice.*

Take predictive policing systems like PredPol. These tools suggest locations for increased police presence based on past crime data. Reform-minded developers might argue that if the input data is diversified—drawn from multiple jurisdictions, cleaned of racial identifiers, or filtered for reliability—the tool becomes less biased. But even under these conditions, PredPol tends to direct police to neighbourhoods that have historically borne the brunt of surveillance. This is because crime reports are not evenly distributed; they reflect unequal patterns of trust in law enforcement, willingness to report, and historical over-policing. The model doesn't just *inherit* bias—it *reifies* it, producing recommendations that look mathematically neutral but are socially regressive.

Data hygiene, in this context, becomes an exercise in aesthetic ethics: it makes systems look cleaner without making them more just. It offers the comfort of "doing something" without addressing the harder, slower work of rethinking what kind of legal systems we want to automate in the first place.

One might imagine a parallel in public health. Imagine designing an AI to triage patients during a pandemic. If the training data systematically underrepresents rural communities or overrepresents hospital patients with insurance, no amount of statistical massaging will make the tool equitable. Its very foundation is uneven. Similarly, in legal AI, cleaning inputs cannot substitute for confronting foundational questions: *Whose experiences are captured? Who defines relevance? Which values are baked into the labels?*

Even more pernicious is the fact that many legal AI systems are trained not only on data, but on *labels*—human-created classifications of what constitutes "success," "risk," "fairness," or "compliance." These are not objective categories. They reflect institutional values and historical norms. A model that flags asylum claims as "low credibility" based on prior adjudications is not learning the truth about asylum-seekers—it is learning the preferences of immigration judges, many of whom operate under political pressure, institutional bias, or sheer case overload. Polishing the data here does not correct the distortion. It merely automates the values already embedded in the system.

Some reformers suggest that algorithmic systems should be "audited" for bias, or that fairness constraints should be baked into model objectives. These are welcome developments, but they too risk being technocratic half-measures. A fairness constraint applied to a discriminatory system is still operating within the bounds of that system. It may equalise outcomes across groups in a statistical sense, but it cannot address *why* those outcomes are being generated in the first place.

Nor can fixing the inputs resolve the *contextual ignorance* of most legal AI systems. Law is not mathematics; its application often hinges on nuance, empathy, moral judgment, and an understanding of lived realities. A bail algorithm may correctly predict that a defendant is statistically more likely to miss a court date, but it cannot account for the fact that she missed her last hearing because she had no childcare or public transport. Clean data will not produce insight into a life it does not understand. The absence is not in the numbers—it is in the narrative.

This epistemic limitation becomes dangerous when AI tools are deployed at scale, especially in high-volume systems like immigration courts, housing tribunals, or public benefits administration. In these contexts, the drive for efficiency often trumps deliberation. Automated systems are rolled out to process thousands of cases quickly, and data cleaning becomes a way to justify speed. But faster injustice is still injustice. Clean inputs cannot save a system designed to prioritise throughput over truth.

There is also a political cost to over-relying on technical fixes. By focusing on data quality, institutions can avoid harder conversations about their own role in generating biased records. They can outsource reform to the tech team while maintaining the same operational logic. This deferral of responsibility is especially appealing in bureaucracies, where accountability is diffuse and inertia is strong. The result is a cycle of cosmetic reform: bias is acknowledged, cleaned, and redeployed—without ever being dismantled.

The alternative requires a shift in mindset. Rather than asking how to fix biased inputs, we must ask *whether the system should be automated at all.* Not every legal task is suitable for algorithmic replication. Not every decision benefits from statistical regularity. Some areas of law—such as juvenile justice, asylum adjudication, or restorative sentencing—may demand forms of reasoning that resist standardisation. In these contexts, *the goal should not be to make AI less biased, but to make human judgment more informed, compassionate, and context-sensitive.*

This does not mean abandoning data-driven tools altogether. But it does mean redefining their role. Rather than replacing discretion, AI should augment it—offering insights while acknowledging its own limits. This requires transparency not just about how models work, but about what they *cannot* do. It means involving diverse stakeholders in the design process, from impacted communities to legal scholars to social workers. And it means resisting the temptation to solve moral problems with technical code.

Ultimately, fixing the inputs is necessary—but never sufficient. Bias is not a contaminant to be filtered out. It is a feature of the systems we've built, the histories we've inherited, and the choices we continue to make. A just legal future will not emerge from cleaner data alone. It will require a deeper reckoning with the structures we are digitising—and a commitment to redesigning them with justice, not just efficiency, as the goal.

Chapter 7
Rethinking Expertise

For centuries, the legal profession rested on a single, unspoken promise: that the craft of interpreting, arguing, and adjudicating law belongs to those trained within its ranks. Licensing, tradition, and institutional gatekeeping reinforced this claim, defining what it meant to be a "lawyer." Yet that definition now faces pressure unlike any before—not from rival professions, but from systems written in code. Machine learning models can summarise legislation, analyse precedent, and predict outcomes faster than a junior associate ever could. Natural language processing tools extract clauses, flag risks, and automate workflows once reserved for experienced practitioners. The pressing question emerges: what, in an age of algorithms, constitutes legal expertise?

The stakes extend beyond careers; they are fundamentally epistemological. Legal work has long been an interpretive craft, a slow and deliberate engagement with ambiguity, context, and language. It requires judgment under uncertainty, an attunement to rhetorical timing, and the capacity to read between lines as much as within them. Yet AI promises to render much of this labour data-driven and "efficient." Discovery becomes text mining; contract review reduces to risk scoring; arguments are modelled in dashboards before ever entering a courtroom. If law can be parsed into logic trees and confidence intervals, what remains of a lawyer's intuition, ethics, or discretion?

One effect of this shift is the migration of legal practice from human craft to procedural compliance. Tasks once bespoke—tailored to clients, circumstances, and evolving norms—are increasingly mapped into rigid workflows. Compliance software flags deviations; algorithmic tools produce templated arguments; predictive engines forecast likely outcomes from historical patterns. This is not merely about saving time; it reshapes the work itself. The lawyer risks being reduced from artisan to system manager, supervising adherence to protocol. Legal thinking, once rich and textured, can flatten into checklist logic—precise and replicable, but stripped of moral and interpretive depth.

This transformation is not abstract. In corporate law departments, legal operations teams collaborate with data scientists to structure workflows. Legal tech startups offer "intelligent" contract review, real-time analytics, and regulatory monitoring—all marketed as ways to speed and standardise legal work. These tools achieve exactly what they promise. Yet their very success highlights a tension: when efficiency dominates, nuance recedes. And where nuance fades, so too does the moral imagination that sustains law's social legitimacy.

Amid this disruption, a new breed of professional emerges—fluent in both law and technology. These "tech-law hybrids" reshape the contours of expertise. Legal engineers write code to automate obligations. Data-literate jurists interrogate the assumptions embedded in machine reasoning. Scholars trained in both AI and jurisprudence build tools that do more than accelerate tasks—they reimagine them. Far from peripheral curiosities, these roles mark the frontier of legal practice. Navigating algorithmic legal systems demands professionals who understand law not only as doctrine, but as data—able to critique, calibrate, and co-create the systems mediating legal power.

Redefining expertise also requires rethinking the skill set. The lawyer of the future cannot rely solely on precedent and persuasion. They must be systems thinkers, pattern recognisers, ethical stewards, and translators across disciplines. They must grasp how algorithms learn, how data distorts, and how automation amplifies inequities—so that they can argue not merely within the law, but about the very frameworks that shape its application. Mastery of rules alone will no longer suffice; legal practitioners must also interrogate the rulebooks, govern the platforms, and steward the datasets through which justice is administered.

Yet the human lawyer is far from obsolete. The enduring value of legal practice may lie precisely in what resists automation: empathy, moral reasoning, contextual judgment. These are not inefficiencies; they are justice's core. In complex cases—where values clash, stakes are deeply personal, or precedent runs thin—speed alone is insufficient. What is required is wisdom: the capacity to sit with ambiguity, to frame the right questions, to consider possibilities as well as answers. No algorithm can replicate that depth. If AI excels at providing answers, human lawyers must excel at asking better questions.

Reclaiming human judgment is not nostalgia—it is strategic necessity. In a world where machines perform much of what junior lawyers once did, the differentiator will be depth of thought rather than speed, interpretive courage rather than procedural compliance. The profession must resist the allure of automation as panacea, cultivating qualities that remain uniquely human: moral clarity, interpretive skill, and the ability to connect legal reasoning to the lived experiences of those it affects.

This chapter explores more than the defence of lawyers' roles; it interrogates the very nature of legal expertise. In an era of automated argumentation and data-driven dispute resolution, we are compelled to envision new forms of authority, pathways into the profession, and responsibilities for those who wield power in law. We are asked not merely to adapt to technology, but to shape it; not merely to preserve law as it was, but to forge a practice worthy of public trust in an increasingly digital age.

The pages ahead chart this transformation with candour and rigor. They question the assumptions underlying legal automation, examine the hybrid roles emerging within the field, and reflect on what constitutes legal wisdom when machines can imitate competence. This is not a story of disruption alone—it is a reawakening of purpose. And it begins with a question no algorithm can answer: what kind of lawyer does justice now require?

What Makes a Lawyer in the Algorithmic Age?

The question once answered by degrees, credentials, and bar memberships must now be rethought in the face of systems that replicate many of the legal profession's most prized capacities. Artificial intelligence is not poised to replace lawyers outright, but it has already begun to erode the exclusive claim they once held over legal expertise. Tasks that were once the bedrock of junior legal work—case research, precedent matching, contract review, litigation risk assessment—can now be performed, in seconds, by software that neither tires nor forgets. The monopoly is cracked. The professional identity is unsettled. *And the urgency to redefine what truly makes someone a "lawyer" has never been greater.*

This shift does not merely signal a redistribution of labour; it challenges the very epistemology of law. Traditionally, legal expertise has rested on the ability to read cases, interpret statutes, reason analogically, and apply abstract principles to concrete facts. But machine learning models are, in some domains, better at detecting patterns than human practitioners—particularly when the goal is predictive rather than interpretive. Software trained on decades of decisions can forecast case outcomes more accurately than seasoned litigators. Risk engines scan compliance documents for red flags in ways that no human could scale. For a profession rooted in precedent and pattern, the arrival of predictive analytics unsettles the old order. *If AI can outperform humans on tasks long considered core to legal reasoning, what distinctive expertise remains in the hands of the lawyer?*

To answer this, we must first distinguish between knowing the law and *doing* law. AI systems excel at retrieving, parsing, and analysing legal data. But they do not—cannot—understand law as a social institution embedded in context, shaped by human conflict, and animated by moral and rhetorical judgment. The essence of law lies not in the rules themselves, but in how they are framed, contested, and adapted to lived realities. A clause in a contract may have a clear linguistic meaning, but its legal import depends on the context of negotiation, the relationship between parties, the surrounding statutory environment, and the interpretive tendencies of a given court. *Legal expertise, at its highest level, is not about rules—it is about framing disputes, constructing meaning, and making judgement calls under uncertainty.*

These are not tasks easily outsourced to algorithms. They require tacit knowledge, emotional intelligence, political awareness, and ethical discernment—qualities that resist codification. And yet, the danger is that in the drive for efficiency and scale, these dimensions are precisely what stand to be devalued. If legal practice is reconceived as document automation, clause extraction, and outcome prediction, then the role of the human lawyer risks becoming merely supervisory: checking outputs, managing software, confirming compliance. The craft of law—its deliberative, argumentative, humanistic core—is hollowed out. *The challenge, then, is not simply to adapt to AI, but to protect and elevate what remains uniquely human within legal reasoning.*

This requires a new skill set—one that bridges the technical and the interpretive. Lawyers must now be literate not only in doctrine, but in data. They must understand how algorithms are trained, where bias creeps in, and how predictive models shape behaviour. Not every lawyer must code. But every lawyer must grasp the assumptions and implications behind the tools they use. When an AI recommends a plea deal based on sentencing data, is it perpetuating past injustices? When software automates discovery, what patterns might it miss because of skewed training sets? These are legal questions, ethical questions, design questions—and the lawyer of the future must be prepared to ask them.

Moreover, the next generation of legal professionals must be collaborators. The archetype of the lone, adversarial litigator is increasingly ill-suited to a world of integrated systems and cross-disciplinary work. Legal teams now routinely include technologists, data scientists, user experience designers, and process engineers. In this landscape, communication across boundaries is not a luxury—it is a necessity. Lawyers must learn to articulate legal values to non-lawyers, translate technical constraints into doctrinal concerns, and work iteratively in environments shaped by constant feedback and testing. *The lawyer is no longer just a legal expert; they are a node in a dynamic ecosystem where law intersects with computation, policy, business, and design.*

This shift is already underway. Legal clinics are partnering with computer science departments. Law schools are offering joint degrees in law and technology. Courts are piloting AI-assisted sentencing tools and dispute resolution platforms. Governments are consulting legal engineers on the design of algorithmic regulation. The profession is expanding, not contracting—but only for those willing to evolve. The lawyer who clings to doctrinal purity without technical fluency may soon find themselves outpaced by hybrid professionals who can traverse both domains.

Yet this evolution must not lapse into technological determinism. The tools may change, but the stakes of law remain human. Justice, fairness, accountability—these are not data points. They are contested ideals that require interpretation, empathy, and advocacy. In this sense, the most essential legal skill in the algorithmic age may be the ability to challenge the assumptions of the system itself. When an AI model denies a benefits claim because the applicant's profile matches a pattern of past denials, it takes a lawyer to ask whether that pattern was just. When a risk assessment tool scores a defendant high because of past arrest records, it takes a lawyer to challenge whether arrest history is an appropriate proxy for danger. *In short, it takes a lawyer to remember that legal systems are not neutral, and that justice is not statistical.*

This is where the profession must reclaim its identity—not as a guild guarding privilege, but as a vocation animated by reasoned argument, moral courage, and democratic accountability. AI may narrow the space for discretionary judgement, but it also reveals how essential that judgement is. The very fact that we now ask what lawyers are for is a reminder of how much the profession once took for granted. The answer, going forward, cannot be tradition or title. It must be substance. Lawyers must justify their place not by claiming superiority, but by demonstrating what only they can offer: the ability to navigate ambiguity, advocate with empathy, reason with context, and fight for fairness when the system forgets how.

Ultimately, the algorithmic age does not spell the end of the legal profession. It marks its next chapter. The old monopoly on expertise is gone—but what remains is a renewed opportunity to define legal excellence not by exclusivity, but by relevance. The question is no longer "Can AI do law?" but "What kind of law do we want to build—and who do we trust to shape it?" The lawyer of tomorrow will not be the keeper of arcane knowledge. They will be the architect of meaning in a world awash with information. *That is not a diminished role. It is a deeper one. And it is one the best lawyers have always been prepared to play.*

From Craft to Compliance

There is a difference—subtle in theory, profound in practice—between legal interpretation and legal execution. One demands judgment; the other, confirmation. Yet in the current wave of technological optimisation sweeping the legal profession, this distinction is steadily collapsing. As AI and workflow automation systems gain traction in everything from contract review to regulatory compliance, the practice of law risks being redefined not as an interpretive craft but as a series of procedural checklists. The promise of speed and consistency is real. But so is the cost: *the flattening of law's conceptual depth into a system of box-ticking where ambiguity becomes a nuisance, not a site of meaning.*

This is not merely a problem of aesthetics or nostalgia for a slower, more artisanal mode of legal practice. It is a structural and epistemic shift. Law, at its best, is an intellectual discipline of argument and counterargument—an ongoing conversation about norms, principles, power, and fairness. It draws strength from its deliberative structure, from its tolerance for competing interpretations, and from the disciplined ambiguity that allows rules to flex when justice demands it. But the very traits that make law robust in the face of human complexity—its interpretability, its nuance, its accommodation of dissent—are the same traits most resistant to automation. *Software thrives on rules. Law survives because not all rules are absolute.*

Compliance software—especially in regulatory-heavy fields like finance, data protection, healthcare, and environmental law—exemplifies this tension. These systems are designed to operationalise statutes and guidelines into workflows, enabling companies to "stay compliant" through automated prompts and alerts. In theory, this ensures consistent adherence to legal norms and reduces human error. In practice, however, it often transforms legal reasoning into a mechanised process where the goal is not to *understand* the law but to *avoid triggering* it. The lawyer becomes a systems manager; the law becomes a set of conditionals.

Consider the case of General Data Protection Regulation (GDPR) compliance platforms. These tools promise turnkey adherence to one of the most sophisticated privacy regimes in the world. Yet many operate on a rules-as-code model, reducing a complex body of jurisprudence into a linear series of form-filling tasks and binary checks. Questions of proportionality, necessity, and legitimate interest—central pillars of European data law—are reduced to simple "yes/no" input fields. The interpretive discretion that once invited legal debate now becomes a risk to be neutralised. *The outcome is compliance without comprehension—legality without legality's meaning.*

Legal departments, often pressured to cut costs and "streamline operations," find this transformation appealing. Document automation, contract lifecycle management tools, and AI-assisted clause suggestion systems promise faster turnaround, fewer bottlenecks, and reduced reliance on costly legal counsel. But speed comes with trade-offs. One major casualty is the erosion of contextual reasoning. Automated workflows may detect anomalies, but they cannot explain them. They may flag deviations, but not advise on when a deviation might be justified. *When law is treated as a system to be executed rather than a discourse to be interpreted, the capacity for principled exception vanishes.*

The trend is reinforced by how legal education and professional expectations are shifting. New lawyers are often trained to "operate" software platforms rather than to challenge their assumptions. They learn to extract precedents, build templates, and manage compliance calendars—but less frequently to question what the law is trying to achieve in the first place. The mastery of legal tools replaces the mastery of legal thought. The result is a profession increasingly defined by its functional efficiency rather than its interpretive sophistication. *What disappears is the notion that law requires moral imagination as much as technical precision.*

This dynamic is particularly concerning in administrative and social welfare adjudication, where automated decision-making systems have been introduced under the banner of efficiency. In countries like the Netherlands and the United Kingdom, benefits eligibility and fraud detection have been partially outsourced to algorithms. These systems process claims based on pre-programmed criteria and risk models, leading to thousands of automatic rejections or sanctions. In theory, human oversight remains. In reality, those checks are often cursory. *The appeal to efficiency cloaks a dangerous abdication of judgment.* When challenged, these systems offer no reasoning—only logs and audit trails. The citizen is reduced to a data profile. The adjudicator becomes a reviewer of machine outputs. And the law is no longer a social contract, but a compliance protocol.

Proponents of automation argue that these systems increase fairness by reducing human bias. But this claim is often overstated and dangerously naive. While automation may remove overt prejudice, it also strips away discretion—the very mechanism by which bias is often corrected. A human adjudicator may choose to show leniency, to contextualise hardship, or to question a rule's applicability. A machine does not. *It can only apply the rule as encoded. It cannot ask whether the rule itself is just.*

Furthermore, the legal profession's embrace of automation is often justified by reference to client demand. In-house counsel and business executives seek predictability and scale. They want to know not just whether something is legal, but whether it can be executed quickly, defensibly, and at minimal cost. In this environment, the lawyer who offers interpretive depth may be seen as a liability—a source of delay, uncertainty, and potential friction. The pressure is not to think harder, but to think faster. Not to question the system, but to feed it. *This is how legal craftsmanship gives way to legal compliance. Not through malice or incompetence, but through optimisation culture disguised as progress.*

Yet the loss is not inevitable. It is the result of choices—often unconscious—about what kind of law we wish to practice, and for whom. There is still space, even within highly technical domains, for legal professionals to resist the drift toward procedural minimalism. It begins with recognising that *not all complexity is inefficiency, and not all ambiguity is a bug.* Some legal questions are hard because they are meant to be—because they reflect competing rights, evolving norms, and contested truths. A good lawyer does not resolve these questions by hiding them behind user interfaces or conditional logic trees. A good lawyer sits with them, argues them, and—when necessary—disrupts them.

To do this, the profession must cultivate a mindset that values interpretation as much as execution. This means resisting the temptation to treat every legal rule as a checklist item. It means designing systems that leave room for judgment, for exception, for human override. It also means training lawyers to understand the tools they use—not merely at the interface level, but at the level of design and assumption. When a contract automation tool suggests a clause, the lawyer must know why that clause was chosen, what risk model supports it, and whether it applies in this context. *The lawyer must remain a craftsperson, not just a technician.*

The way forward is not to reject technology, but to embed it within a richer understanding of legal practice. Tools should augment human judgment, not replace it. Automation should handle the rote so that the human mind is freed for the interpretive. And systems should be designed not merely to minimise legal exposure, but to support legal deliberation. This requires a shift in how we value legal work. If the worth of a lawyer is measured solely by output speed and error minimisation, then machines will win. But if worth is measured by insight, courage, and the ability to navigate moral and legal complexity, the human lawyer remains indispensable.

Ultimately, the legal system does not need more efficient checkbox tickers. It needs professionals capable of discerning when the box itself is flawed—when the checklist omits what matters, when the rule misfires, and when the system's logic must yield to the deeper demands of justice. That kind of discernment is not programmable. It is learned through practice, nurtured by culture, and sustained by a commitment to law not merely as code, but as a living craft. *To forget this is to trade the soul of the legal profession for the ghost of efficiency. To remember it is to insist that law remains a human art—even when rendered in lines of code.*

The Rise of the Tech-Law Hybrid

It is no longer sufficient for lawyers to only know the law. Increasingly, they must know the systems through which the law is delivered, interpreted, and operationalised—and that means engaging with technology not as a peripheral tool, but as a central pillar of legal infrastructure. As artificial intelligence reshapes everything from contract review to sentencing algorithms, a new breed of legal professional is emerging: the tech-law hybrid. These are not merely lawyers who use software, nor technologists with a passing interest in regulation. They are interdisciplinary actors—legal engineers, computational jurists, regulatory designers—who bridge the traditional divide between code and jurisprudence. *They are not just translating legal questions into technical problems. They are redefining the boundaries of what legal expertise means in a digitised world.*

This shift is not cosmetic. It marks a structural transformation in the architecture of legal authority. For centuries, legal power was held by those who mastered precedent, rhetoric, and doctrinal nuance. In the algorithmic age, that power is shared—sometimes uncomfortably—with those who can structure data, map logic, and write the rules that machines will follow. Legal norms, once expressed in prose and refined through case law, are increasingly embedded in code—automating decisions about eligibility, compliance, liability, and even risk. In this environment, the question is no longer just *what does the law say?*, but *how is the law being operationalised in machine-readable logic—and by whom?*

Consider the case of legal engineers—professionals trained in both law and computer science, often working within law firms, tech companies, or governmental bodies. Their job is not to argue cases, but to build systems. They design contract automation platforms, regulatory compliance engines, and knowledge management tools that encode legal reasoning into dynamic workflows. They structure decision trees, craft if-then logic models, and advise on how statutory text can be translated into machine-executable formats. *In doing so, they shape not just legal processes, but legal outcomes.*

The rise of these hybrid roles is both a response to and a driver of institutional change. Major international firms now host internal teams of technologists, data scientists, and legal process architects tasked with reimagining service delivery. The Big Four accounting firms—Deloitte, PwC, EY, and KPMG—are investing heavily in legal technology platforms, betting that scalable automation will become a key differentiator in the regulatory space. Meanwhile, courts and public agencies are adopting AI tools to assist with document classification, docket prioritisation, and early-stage dispute resolution. *Across all these domains, the capacity to build and audit systems is becoming as important as the capacity to argue doctrine.*

One telling example comes from the United Kingdom's HM Courts and Tribunals Service (HMCTS), which launched an ambitious court modernisation programme aimed at digitising everything from filing to case tracking. While traditional lawyers focused on ensuring procedural compliance, a parallel cadre of designers, developers, and policy technologists worked behind the scenes to translate legal rules into user-friendly digital interfaces. They decided what defaults to set, what questions to ask, and how legal categories would be presented. These design choices, though technical on the surface, had profound legal implications. They shaped how litigants understood their options, how evidence was submitted, and how cases progressed. *In essence, the system was redesigned not just as a service, but as a gatekeeper of justice—and the people doing the redesign were not exclusively lawyers.*

This raises pressing questions about accountability, legitimacy, and the distribution of expertise. If a software platform recommends a certain clause in a contract, is it offering legal advice? If a regulatory dashboard flags a firm's compliance risk based on internal data analytics, who is responsible for interpreting or acting on that signal? If a public benefits algorithm denies someone support based on inferred eligibility, what recourse do they have—and against whom? *The traditional boundaries between legal counsel, technological interface, and institutional authority are blurring—and the consequences are far from trivial.*

These tensions are especially acute in jurisdictions experimenting with rules-as-code—an approach that treats legal text not as interpretive prose, but as programmable logic. Governments in Australia, New Zealand, and parts of the EU have piloted projects in which statutes are drafted or published in both human-readable and machine-readable formats, enabling real-time feedback, automated compliance tools, and policy simulation. This is not merely a back-end upgrade. It represents a fundamental shift in how laws are conceived, deployed, and enforced. *Those who can write the code that governs interpretation—whether in the public or private sector—wield outsized power over how laws are experienced in practice.*

Not all reactions to this shift have been enthusiastic. Many traditionalists fear that the rise of tech-law hybrids dilutes the normative and deliberative function of legal practice. They worry that by privileging efficiency, structure, and automation, these roles risk turning law into a sterile exercise in logic, severed from the messy realities of social life. There is truth in that concern. *Law is not engineering, and treating it as such can strip away the humanistic and contextual dimensions that give it moral weight.*

But the counterpoint is equally important. In a world governed increasingly by technical systems—credit scoring algorithms, content moderation platforms, automated hiring tools—*the failure to engage technically is not a principled stand. It is a surrender.* Lawyers who cannot understand the systems through which rules are enacted will become marginal to the institutions they once guided. Worse, they may unwittingly endorse systems they do not comprehend, or over-trust outputs they cannot verify.

This is why the emergence of data-literate jurists is not a novelty but a necessity. These are professionals who understand that legal reasoning and technical reasoning are not mutually exclusive, and that each can inform the other. They know how to interrogate an algorithmic decision process not just for technical robustness, but for legal justification. They can spot where a data model's outputs may conflict with due process or equal protection. And they can articulate those concerns in ways that both engineers and judges can understand. *They are translators across disciplines—and in many contexts, they are the only ones capable of keeping systems both efficient and just.*

Training such professionals requires a rethink of both legal education and organisational culture. Law schools must integrate courses on logic, computation, ethics of technology, and regulatory design—not as electives, but as core competencies. Firms must recognise that the best teams are not siloed, but collaborative—composed of people who can navigate across professional grammars. Regulatory agencies must develop new evaluative frameworks that incorporate both legal reasoning and technical auditability. And judges, too, must be equipped to understand the systems they are asked to rely on, critique, or authorise.

This is not about everyone becoming a coder. It is about developing *conceptual bilingualism*—a capacity to reason fluently about law *and* systems. It is about understanding that a clause is not just text but data, that a rule is not just a norm but a structure, and that a legal system is not just a forum but an infrastructure. The rise of the tech-law hybrid is a signal that the profession is entering a new phase—

one in which legal authority is distributed, interdependent, and as much about design as about doctrine.

Whether this shift leads to empowerment or erosion depends on how seriously it is taken. If treated as a sideshow, it will deepen divides and hand over control to technologists unburdened by legal ethics. If embraced with rigour, it offers a way forward—a model of legal practice that is more attuned to the systems shaping modern life, more responsive to change, and more capable of keeping law a living, dynamic, and human enterprise. *The future of legal expertise will not be written solely in statutes or courtrooms. Increasingly, it will be encoded in systems—and those who can read, write, and challenge those systems will define what law means in the algorithmic age.*

Reclaiming Human Judgment as a Competitive Edge

It is telling that in the legal industry's race toward automation, the most undervalued quality may be the one that should never have been negotiable: *human judgment.* While artificial intelligence excels at pattern recognition, statistical inference, and rapid processing of vast datasets, it falters—systematically and predictably—in the face of ambiguity, moral nuance, and the social texture of lived experience. These are not peripheral to legal practice. They are *its essence.* Yet as law firms and courts rush to adopt machine-driven solutions in search of speed and scale, they risk displacing the very thing that makes law a human institution rather than a mechanical process.

What is emerging, ironically, is an opportunity: the rediscovery of judgment as a *strategic advantage.* As automation flattens complex decisions into risk scores and compliance trees, those who can see what machines miss—who can recognise when formal logic fails to capture contextual meaning—will not be relics of a fading profession. They will be its future. The distinguishing lawyer in the algorithmic age will not be the one who memorises precedent faster than a search engine, but the one who understands when precedent is *wrongly applied, misaligned with justice, or blind to social consequence.* This is not romanticism; it is realism in a world where machine-made law is only as good as the data it consumes—and the humans who still must interpret its results.

Take, for instance, a common scenario in algorithmically assisted bail decisions. Risk-assessment tools like COMPAS, widely used in the United States, assign a numerical score to indicate the likelihood that a defendant will reoffend or fail to appear in court. These scores are calculated using factors such as age, employment history, and prior arrests. But they do not account for whether those arrests were the result of discriminatory policing, nor do they consider the specific circumstances of the accused—family obligations, health concerns, or a credible job offer starting next week. *What appears as statistical objectivity is in fact a flattening of human complexity into generic variables.* The judge who defers entirely to the score relinquishes the duty to weigh meaningfully. The judge who challenges or contextualises it reclaims the role of justice as discernment.

The legal profession must now assert the distinct value of what machines cannot do: reason through ambiguity, grapple with competing principles, and navigate conflicts not resolvable through optimisation. Consider 'how legal questions often pivot on interpretation rather than calculation. What constitutes "reasonable doubt" or "fair use" cannot be reduced to numeric thresholds. These are inherently contextual judgements, shaped by evolving norms, particular facts, and the delicate calibration of values. *They require a human mind willing to deliberate, not simply execute.*

This is not to suggest that machines have no place in legal decision-making. Their analytical capabilities are unmatched in detecting patterns across volumes of data no human could read in a lifetime. They reveal consistencies, inconsistencies, and potential correlations that might otherwise go unnoticed. But what they reveal *requires interpretation.* They can tell us where anomalies lie; they cannot tell us whether those anomalies are errors, injustices, or necessary exceptions. They can flag inconsistencies in sentencing, but they cannot explain why two cases that look similar on paper may differ in the significance of context. And they certainly cannot make peace between competing moral claims.

In complex legal practice—where relationships, emotions, and reputations are at stake—*relational judgment* becomes indispensable. A client may ask whether a course of action is lawful, but they often mean something more: Is it wise? Is it justifiable in the public eye?

Will it strengthen or damage trust with key stakeholders? These are questions of ethics, perception, and consequence. No algorithm, however sophisticated, is equipped to answer them. Lawyers who can offer such counsel—grounded in experience, cultural awareness, and ethical reflection—will command trust in a way that no tool can replicate.

There is also an institutional dimension to this argument. Legal systems do not function solely on efficiency. They depend on legitimacy—on the belief that outcomes are fair, deliberative, and responsive to the particularities of each case. If citizens feel they are being judged by machines rather than understood by humans, confidence in the justice system will erode. Transparency, empathy, and responsiveness to context are not bureaucratic luxuries; they are the scaffolding of democratic legitimacy. *Human judgment is not an obstacle to justice. It is the medium through which justice is rendered visible.*

To be clear, this is not a nostalgic appeal to preserve an elite profession from technological encroachment. It is a call for intellectual clarity about what machines are good at—and where they fail. The danger is not that AI will replace lawyers. The danger is that lawyers will behave as if they are machines, reducing their craft to checklist compliance, risk modelling, or automated reasoning. When lawyers internalise the values of automation—speed, standardisation, optimisation—they risk losing the very disposition that makes legal practice humane: the capacity to dwell in uncertainty, to entertain competing narratives, to admit doubt, and to seek wisdom rather than precision.

The task ahead is not simply to defend human judgment, but to *develop* it—to treat it as a skill, not a given. That means rethinking legal education. Law schools must teach not only doctrine and logic, but ethical reasoning, cross-cultural awareness, and the psychology of decision-making. Case studies should focus not just on legal correctness, but on the *quality* of the judgments rendered—how well they balanced competing interests, how they were received by affected communities, how they evolved in light of new evidence. Mentorship, too, becomes critical. Judgment is not taught through lectures; it is cultivated through exposure to wise practitioners, complex cases, and the reflective habit of asking *why* a particular decision was right—not just legally, but morally and socially.

Firms and institutions must also reward judgment, not just output. Billable hours and performance metrics must give way to more qualitative indicators of professional value—client trust, team leadership, insight under pressure, and ethical courage. These are not intangible. They are often the difference between long-term success and short-term expediency. In complex regulatory environments, in high-stakes litigation, and in public service, *the lawyer who can navigate uncertainty with poise and principle will be indispensable.*

This reframing does not deny the power of AI. It contextualises it. Machines are powerful precisely because they are not like us. But because they are not like us, they *need* us—to guide them, to correct them, and, sometimes, to resist them. The lawyer's role in the algorithmic age is not to compete with machines at their own game, but to play a different game: one of interpretation, discernment, and wisdom. The value of human judgment is not diminished by technology. It is *made more visible by contrast.*

The legal systems of the future will be hybrid ecosystems—part data-driven, part human-led. Those who thrive will be those who understand both parts, but who never forget which part holds moral responsibility. Law is not just about rules. It is about people. And people are not algorithms. They are complex, contradictory, and vulnerable. *To serve them well is to embrace the very complexity that machines cannot grasp—and to reclaim judgment not just as a relic of the past, but as the most vital asset we bring to the future.*

Chapter 8
Governance Without Consent

No one cast a vote for the algorithm that decides which taxpayers face audits. No parliamentary debate preceded the introduction of a proprietary sentencing tool in criminal courts. No constitutional amendment authorised foreign-designed legal software to mediate land disputes in rural Africa. Yet all of these scenarios are unfolding in reality. The expansion of legal technology has quietly remade governance, shifting the locus of authority from elected deliberation to lines of code. This is not a theoretical concern; it is happening now, and at a pace far swifter than democratic processes can track—or respond to.

The allure of legal automation lies in its promise of order, efficiency, and scalability, particularly in systems long burdened by delay and discretionary overload. But embedded within this promise is a subtle inversion of power. AI systems do not merely assist existing frameworks; they increasingly become the framework itself. Human judgment is supplanted by automated logic, and design choices made by private developers replace collective deliberation. In practice, this produces policy without politics, enforcement without oversight, and control without consent.

The pattern is familiar: legal technologies are deployed far ahead of regulatory frameworks. Facial recognition for policing, algorithmic triage for immigration, or fraud detection in social welfare systems are rolled out with minimal scrutiny and maximal confidence. These tools often operate in legal grey zones, where private vendors define the boundaries of governmental action. Frequently, code arrives first, consequences follow, and legislation limps along years later—if it arrives at all. The rule of law, in effect, is being rewritten not by elected representatives but by software engineers and procurement offices.

The implications are profound. Law has traditionally functioned not only as an instrument of order but also as a medium for collective reasoning, a shared language for negotiating justice, fairness, and power. Legal automation threatens to short-circuit that conversation. When decisions are embedded in proprietary algorithms shielded by intellectual property, transparency is not merely reduced—it is structurally foreclosed. Citizens may face determinations they cannot scrutinise, contest, or even comprehend. Democracy struggles to survive when its rules are hidden behind trade secrets.

Commercial imperatives compound this opacity. Systems such as COMPAS, which assesses risk among criminal defendants in the United States, or HMRC's Connect system in the United Kingdom, are often developed and maintained by private companies whose accountability is to shareholders, not the public. Yet these tools now shape law not as advisors but as gatekeepers. Their scalability and purported objectivity allow influence to expand rapidly, often without public notice or debate.

Beyond national borders, legal technology has become a subtle instrument of geopolitical influence. AI systems designed in the Global North—Silicon Valley, London, Beijing—are exported under the banner of modernisation to justice systems in the Global South. These tools carry assumptions about property, crime, and family life that reflect the priorities of their designers, rather than the cultural and legal norms of the communities affected. The result is a form of digital colonialism: legal architectures imposed without local consultation or consent, presenting technological progress as neutral while masking embedded power dynamics.

Consider Kenya's experience with blockchain-based land registries, introduced to combat fraud and inefficiency. International donors praised the innovation, yet local communities reported that it ignored traditional stewardship practices, failed to accommodate collective ownership, and advantaged those literate in formal law. The system was not more equitable; it was more exclusionary, legitimised by the aura of digital sophistication yet disconnected from social reality. Similar patterns are visible across Latin America, Southeast Asia, and sub-Saharan Africa, where imported AI solutions risk compressing complex legal pluralism into algorithmic uniformity.

The problem is deeper than design flaws; it is conceptual. Legal technology is often framed as a tool for executing law efficiently. But law is not a spreadsheet to be run; it is a conversation, evolving through contestation, negotiation, and interpretation. Introducing AI without mechanisms for democratic input freezes that conversation and privileges the worldview of its creators. Deploying such tools without consent is not a minor oversight—it is a profound democratic failure. Governance without deliberation is not governance; it is control.

What is urgently required is a new social contract for legal AI, one that prioritises consent, transparency, and accountability from the outset. Innovation need not be rejected, but it must be anchored in legitimacy. Predictive models used to determine asylum eligibility must be subject to scrutiny, challenge, and ethical review. Tax algorithms must be intelligible and contestable. Sentencing tools must reflect not only codified rules but also community values. The deployment of technology in law must be democratically authorised, not merely technically feasible.

This demands a reassertion of democratic authority over technical systems. Legislators, regulators, and civil society must cultivate the capacity to interrogate AI not merely for bias or efficiency, but for normative alignment. Which values are encoded? Who benefits? Who bears the risks? Who decides when the system should be retired? These are constitutional questions, not engineering ones, and engineers alone cannot answer them.

Building this capacity requires new institutions: auditing bodies with expertise in law, technology, and ethics; public forums for participatory oversight; procurement standards mandating transparency and user control; and accountability frameworks that ensure reparations when systems fail. Such structures must be anticipatory, not reactive, because once an AI system produces harm, its effects are often systemic, entrenched, and irreversible.

The path forward is neither a retreat to manual processes nor blind faith in automation. It requires a principled reevaluation of how power is embedded in code, and how law can reclaim its status as a public good rather than a commercial product. Consent—not efficiency—must sit at the heart of technological governance. Speed without scrutiny is coercion; legitimacy is the precondition for power, not a byproduct.

When used responsibly, legal AI can expand access to justice, streamline bureaucracy, and enhance decision-making. But only if it is shaped by those it governs. Governance without consent is not innovation—it is usurpation. The real question for the digital state is not whether we can build systems to govern, but whether we retain the authority and responsibility to govern the systems we create.

When Legal Tech Bypasses Regulation

In 2014, a predictive policing tool called PredPol was deployed in several American cities, claiming to forecast future crime locations based on historical data. It was marketed as a neutral, objective instrument that could help law enforcement allocate resources more efficiently. Few questioned its technical design, and even fewer understood its implications. Yet within a year, investigations revealed that the system was disproportionately sending officers into poor, predominantly Black neighbourhoods—not because these areas were more crime-ridden, but because historical policing practices had created a feedback loop of over-surveillance. The tool did not predict crime. It predicted where police had previously chosen to look. And it operated without any formal regulatory approval, ethical review, or public debate. *A software update was governing lives without a legislative mandate.*

This is not an isolated case. Across domains—from social welfare screening to immigration control, sentencing, taxation, housing eligibility, and public benefits—AI-driven systems are quietly reshaping state functions. They are not just assisting decision-makers. They are often making the decisions themselves. And in doing so, they routinely *outrun the regulatory frameworks* that would normally constrain such powers. Unlike pharmaceuticals, aircraft, or food additives, there is no mandatory pre-approval regime for algorithmic governance tools. The prevailing logic is "deploy first, regulate later"—a logic that reverses the very principle of legality on which democratic systems depend.

At the heart of this phenomenon lies a structural mismatch between the speed of technological development and the deliberative nature of legal reform. AI developers iterate rapidly, often releasing tools within months of initial conception. Legislators, by contrast, operate on timelines shaped by consultation, compromise, and constitutional process. This disparity creates a policy lag—a window during which unregulated systems can exert significant influence before oversight mechanisms are even imagined. In that window, private actors effectively shape public policy through code.

The implications are particularly acute in legal contexts, where decisions bear directly on individual rights, liberties, and status under the law. Consider the use of AI in asylum adjudication. Several governments, including Canada and the United Kingdom, have experimented with automated systems to triage or even assess claims. But asylum law is not a straightforward application of rules; it requires contextual interpretation, cultural literacy, and sensitivity to the politics of persecution. When automation bypasses these human judgments, the result is not simply administrative efficiency—it is the erosion of discretion in precisely the places where it matters most. *Regulatory delay becomes a form of structural injustice.*

The private sector's role further complicates the landscape. Many legal tech tools are developed by for-profit companies whose motivations are commercial rather than civic. These firms are not bound by constitutional duties, nor are they subject to the transparency obligations that govern public institutions. Yet their systems are often embedded within public agencies, from courts to revenue services, in ways that make them de facto lawmakers. The codebase becomes a shadow statute—unchangeable by courts, unreadable by citizens, and exempt from democratic challenge. This is *governance without visibility*, let alone consent.

Intellectual property protections exacerbate the problem. Vendors frequently refuse to disclose the inner workings of their algorithms, citing trade secrets. This makes it virtually impossible for oversight bodies, let alone affected individuals, to audit the fairness or legality of the decisions being made. When a New York judge sought to review the proprietary risk scores produced by a sentencing algorithm, the software company refused. The result: *a system that can determine a person's freedom operates without public accountability, shielded by commercial privilege.*

Even well-intentioned deployments can create cascading harms when regulation is absent. In the Netherlands, the SyRI system—designed to detect welfare fraud using predictive analytics—was ultimately struck down by the courts for violating privacy rights and creating discriminatory outcomes. But only after years of quiet operation during which vulnerable populations were surveilled, interrogated, and penalised. In hindsight, the problem was not the intention of the tool but its unregulated implementation. The system functioned in the shadows until its harms reached the threshold of public scandal. *By the time oversight arrives, damage is often deeply entrenched.*

Some governments have begun to recognise the urgency of the issue. The European Union's proposed AI Act is a notable attempt to establish ex-ante safeguards, requiring high-risk systems to undergo rigorous testing, documentation, and human oversight before deployment. But even this legislation faces challenges: determining what qualifies as "high-risk," ensuring enforcement across diverse member states, and preventing regulatory capture by industry interests. Meanwhile, outside the EU, most jurisdictions still lack a coherent framework for assessing or authorising legal AI tools. The United States, for example, relies largely on sectoral guidelines and voluntary compliance. In practice, *the gap between technical capacity and regulatory maturity remains dangerously wide.*

The consequences are not only legal but democratic. When legal functions are automated without oversight, the locus of power shifts from public forums to private servers. Citizens no longer know where decisions are made or by whom. They cannot appeal to elected officials, because the officials themselves may not understand—or even be aware of—the tools being used. Judicial review becomes futile if the reasoning behind an administrative decision is inaccessible. And public trust erodes when governance feels opaque, unaccountable, and imposed. *The legitimacy of law depends not only on its content but on its process. Regulation is not bureaucracy; it is what makes power lawful.*

Some argue that the regulatory vacuum is simply a symptom of innovation outpacing institutions. But that framing understates the stakes. Legal tech is not like ride-sharing or food delivery—its consequences are existential. It determines who is eligible for health care, who is incarcerated, who is deported, who receives benefits, who can vote, and who is watched. The claim that regulation should "catch up later" presumes that harm is acceptable so long as it is novel. It presumes that rights can be suspended in the name of optimisation. It *confuses speed with progress.*

Moreover, the notion that technical systems are value-neutral has enabled policymakers to outsource moral decisions to engineers. In practice, design choices encode political assumptions: what constitutes fraud, how to measure risk, what features to consider, and what outcomes to prioritise. These are not mere engineering problems. They are questions of justice. And they require the kind of public reasoning that only regulatory frameworks can provide. *To govern technology is to govern the values embedded within it.*

Rebalancing this dynamic will not be easy. It requires more than retroactive audits or scattered ethical guidelines. It demands a *structural commitment to anticipatory governance*—to building institutions capable of evaluating systems before they are embedded, and of revising or revoking those systems when they fall short. That means equipping regulators with technical expertise, statutory authority, and political independence. It means mandating transparency as a condition of procurement, not a retrospective courtesy. It means treating automated legal tools as instruments of power—not as products to be purchased, but as policies to be debated.

It also demands civic engagement. Citizens must be informed participants in the debate over legal tech, not passive subjects. They must be able to understand how systems work, how to challenge them, and how to shape their development. This requires public education, journalistic scrutiny, and access to meaningful redress. It requires governments to see the public not as users of digital services, but as *owners of democratic governance.*

Ultimately, regulation is not an obstacle to innovation. It is what separates innovation from imposition. It is the mechanism through which society decides what technologies are worth deploying—and on what terms. When legal tech bypasses regulation, it bypasses that conversation. It seizes the power of law without assuming its responsibilities. And in doing so, it undermines the very system it purports to improve. *If democracy is to remain viable in the algorithmic age, the law must not be coded without consent.*

Private Code, Public Consequences

In 2016, Eric Loomis was sentenced in a Wisconsin courtroom not just by a judge, but by a proprietary algorithm. The software—COMPAS, developed by a private company—had evaluated Loomis's likelihood of reoffending and produced a risk score that weighed heavily in the judge's decision. Loomis's legal team sought to challenge the score but were denied access to the algorithm's internal workings. The company claimed its code was a trade secret. The court upheld the sentence. A black-box system, owned and operated by a private entity, had materially shaped a public decision about liberty—and neither the defendant nor the judiciary could peer inside it.

This event is no aberration. From criminal justice to tax enforcement, welfare eligibility to housing allocations, governments around the world are increasingly integrating privately developed algorithms into the machinery of law. These systems do not merely assist public officials; they *define* outcomes. And yet, they often operate beyond public scrutiny, shielded by commercial confidentiality. The paradox is stark: decisions once made through democratic deliberation and subject to legal appeal are now embedded in proprietary code, immune to public challenge. *We are living with the public consequences of private design.*

The allure of algorithmic efficiency is understandable. Legal systems, overburdened and underfunded, are drawn to automation as a solution to backlog, inconsistency, and human error. Companies offer software that promises speed, objectivity, and scalability. But these tools are not deployed in a vacuum—they enter complex institutional ecologies, where their assumptions, limitations, and priorities carry weight. When an algorithm classifies a benefit applicant as high-risk or flags a tax return for fraud investigation, it initiates a chain of consequences that are often difficult to contest. And when the logic behind those classifications is hidden behind a contractual firewall, *transparency becomes an aspiration, not a guarantee.*

Consider the Dutch welfare scandal known as the "Toeslagenaffaire." Over 20,000 families—many of immigrant background—were falsely accused of benefit fraud by a semi-automated system used by the Dutch Tax Authority. The algorithm disproportionately targeted ethnic minorities, but the internal logic remained opaque until investigative journalism and legal activism exposed it. The result was not only a political crisis but a human one: families driven into debt, children removed from their homes, and careers destroyed. This was not a failure of public policy alone; it was a failure of governance *outsourced to code.*

The deeper issue lies in the mismatch between private incentives and public obligations. Commercial developers of legal tech tools are not bound by constitutional principles. They are accountable to shareholders, not citizens. Their goals include profit, market expansion, and IP protection—not due process or equal protection under the law. Yet their systems increasingly *stand in* for legal judgment, functioning as hidden legislators. The danger is not that machines are replacing judges, but that corporations are *defining the terms of judgment without democratic mandate.*

Even where governments seek oversight, they often lack the technical expertise to interrogate complex models. Procurement officers are not machine learning experts. Civil servants may not understand how a neural network processes inputs or why it produces particular outputs. Vendors, meanwhile, claim that their models are proprietary, too complex to explain, or both. This asymmetry of knowledge and power reduces accountability to a formality. Public officials may believe they are retaining final authority, but in practice, they defer to systems they cannot audit. *Deference becomes delegation, and delegation becomes abdication.*

This tension becomes especially salient in sentencing, where the stakes involve years of human life. Risk assessment tools like COMPAS, LSI-R, and Public Safety Assessment (PSA) are used to determine bail, parole, and sentencing conditions. Yet multiple studies have shown that these systems can replicate or even amplify racial disparities. The problem is not merely the data—though historical bias is often baked into the training sets—but the opacity of the systems themselves. Judges are encouraged to consider scores without understanding their derivation. Defendants have no meaningful way to contest them. The result is a jurisprudence *dictated by code, unexaminable and unaccountable.*

The problem extends to tax systems, where algorithms screen for fraud, trigger audits, and flag suspicious returns. In the United Kingdom, the HMRC has piloted AI-based risk models to optimise enforcement. But when such models disproportionately scrutinise low-income earners or self-employed individuals without transparency, they raise critical questions: Who designed the risk parameters? What trade-offs were made between false positives and false negatives? Were any communities unfairly burdened? The answers are often unavailable—not just to the public, but to the agencies themselves. *The epistemology of public law is now dependent on corporate epistemics.*

Defenders of proprietary systems argue that intellectual property protection is necessary to incentivise innovation. Without the ability to protect code, companies might hesitate to invest in complex tools for public use. But this claim must be weighed against democratic imperatives. The state is not a customer like any other. When it adopts a technology to exercise legal authority, that tool becomes part of the state's power. If the source code cannot be scrutinised, challenged, or reformed, then that power is *unmoored from democratic legitimacy.*

The analogy to pharmaceuticals is instructive. Drug companies are permitted to protect formulations—but only after submitting to rigorous testing, peer review, and regulatory approval. No medication reaches the public without detailed disclosure of risks and mechanisms. Why should legal technologies—whose consequences are no less grave—be held to a lower standard? The answer is not to outlaw proprietary code altogether, but to establish conditions under which it can be used: mandatory audits, explainability standards, adversarial testing, and public registers of algorithmic tools. *A public function should not depend on a black box.*

One promising direction is the emergence of algorithmic impact assessments—structured evaluations that consider how a given system will affect rights, due process, and social equity. But these tools remain nascent and often lack enforcement power. To make them meaningful, they must be backed by legal requirements, institutional expertise, and the right of affected individuals to demand review. Transparency should not be a favour granted by vendors. It should be a *condition of public procurement.*

It is also time to rethink procurement practices themselves. Governments should not be passive consumers of legal tech. They should be co-designers, demanding systems that reflect public values and retain human interpretive control. This means rejecting tools that cannot be interrogated. It means prioritising explainability over efficiency. It means involving legal scholars, ethicists, and affected communities in development and deployment. *Public consequences require public authorship.*

The broader philosophical point is this: the law is not merely a set of outputs. It is a *process*—a way of interpreting rules, balancing principles, and responding to context. When this process is encoded by private entities, without oversight or challenge, we lose something more than transparency. We lose the ability to shape the law as a collective project. We outsource not just decisions, but *decision-making itself.* In doing so, we dilute the meaning of legal citizenship.

This is not a Luddite argument. Technology has a legitimate role in modernising public administration. But it must be harnessed with care. The promise of legal AI lies not in replacing human judgment but in *supporting it through tools that are accountable, intelligible, and subject to public control.* Anything less is not innovation. It is a silent reconfiguration of sovereignty.

In the end, the legitimacy of public law depends not only on the fairness of outcomes, but on the openness of process. When code becomes law, it must answer to the people. When it doesn't, it ceases to be law at all—and becomes merely *power, automated.*

Global Inequality by Design

In 2020, Rwanda announced a partnership with an international legal tech company to digitise its judiciary—ostensibly to modernise courts, expedite case resolution, and improve transparency. At face value, this move aligned with global calls for judicial efficiency. Yet, the software deployed was modelled on Euro-American norms: adversarial litigation processes, formal evidentiary rules, and English-based interfaces that did not reflect local custom or linguistic practice. Judges unfamiliar with the new logic were trained not to question it, but to operate it. Over time, legal reasoning itself began to shift—not through public debate or democratic consent, but via the silent logic of an imported machine. This is *modernisation by code*, and with it comes a new frontier of asymmetry: technological hegemony dressed in the language of progress.

As artificial intelligence becomes an instrument of governance, its spread is not ideologically neutral. Legal AI systems exported from the Global North increasingly define the architecture of justice in the Global South. These tools—whether in the form of digital courts, predictive analytics, or compliance platforms—embed the epistemologies and institutional biases of their origin. Yet they are often adopted wholesale, under pressure to keep pace with innovation, comply with donor requirements, or attract investment. *What results is not localisation, but legal displacement: the quiet override of plural legal traditions in favour of computational mimicry of Western norms.*

This phenomenon is not new. Colonial powers once imposed legal codes that disregarded indigenous dispute resolution and customary practice. Today, the agents are different—Silicon Valley startups, European consultancies, international development agencies—but the mechanism is hauntingly familiar. What was once done with ink and statute is now done with code and interface. The language has changed—"efficiency," "interoperability," "capacity building"—but the effect remains: *foreign ideas dictate local outcomes.*

Consider the use of AI in immigration and border control, where biometric databases, risk-scoring systems, and surveillance tools developed in Europe are now being deployed in African and South Asian states through donor-funded "capacity enhancement" programmes. These technologies are often embedded in legal regimes with few safeguards, limited data protection laws, and weak judicial review. The power dynamic is structural: countries dependent on foreign aid or infrastructure loans are offered systems as "gifts"—but the operational logic, ownership rights, and algorithmic assumptions remain opaque. Sovereignty is traded for functionality. *Modernisation becomes a Trojan horse.*

The legal systems these technologies alter are not blank slates. Many developing countries host hybrid legal orders—common law layered over customary law, Islamic jurisprudence alongside secular codes, oral traditions within statutory frameworks. These systems evolved in context: culturally embedded, linguistically diverse, and socially negotiated. Yet AI systems require clean data, standardised categories, and formalised rules. The messiness of legal pluralism is treated not as a feature, but a bug. The result is a form of *algorithmic flattening*—where nuance, discretion, and cultural specificity are erased to make room for machine readability.

This is not merely a technical issue. It is a political one. When dispute resolution tools no longer reflect community norms, trust in legal institutions declines. When compliance models criminalise practices that were once socially sanctioned, marginalisation deepens. When foreign companies control the terms of access to public legal systems—via licensing fees, support contracts, or software dependencies—*justice becomes a subscription service.* The formal appearance of legality remains, but the centre of gravity has shifted. Local judges, lawyers, and litigants must navigate systems they did not design, cannot alter, and do not own.

There are real-world consequences to this dynamic. In Kenya, a pilot programme introduced digital case management tools in family courts. While intended to streamline divorce proceedings, the system only supported nuclear family definitions and excluded traditional polygamous relationships, effectively rendering certain customary marriages invisible. In India, automated tax compliance tools promoted by international consultancies assumed regular wage income and digital literacy, disadvantaging millions of informal workers. In Brazil, facial recognition surveillance for public safety—outsourced to foreign firms—was disproportionately deployed in favelas, reinforcing racialised policing under the banner of "smart justice." *In each case, technology did not merely improve the system—it redefined who the system was for.*

Supporters of global legal tech deployment often invoke a benevolent rationale: digital tools will reduce corruption, increase efficiency, and standardise justice. But these goals mask deeper tensions. Who defines corruption? What does efficiency mean in a context where relational dispute settlement may take time but preserve social harmony? What is standardisation when communities value difference over uniformity? These are not just policy questions. They are *jurisprudential choices*, now being made by software architects and data scientists far removed from the societies affected.

The asymmetry is not just between North and South, but between public need and private control. Companies providing legal AI solutions often retain ownership over the data generated, limiting state access to analytics or model refinement. Local developers are sidelined in procurement processes. And crucially, affected populations are rarely consulted about what kind of justice system they want. The model of governance here is not participatory—it is extractive. *Data flows north, while decision-making moves out of reach.*

This structural imbalance is compounded by language. English dominates the AI legal tech ecosystem—not only in code, but in documentation, training, and interface design. Multilingual legal systems struggle to integrate tools that cannot parse indigenous languages or dialects. Translation is often superficial, and the deeper grammar of culture is lost. As a result, the very accessibility promised by legal tech becomes a barrier. A system that cannot speak your language cannot understand your rights. A system that cannot interpret your norms cannot fairly adjudicate your claims.

What emerges is not a level playing field but a digitally tiered world. Wealthy jurisdictions design, test, and export. Low-income states adapt, absorb, and endure. But this is not inevitable. It is the result of choices—about funding priorities, procurement standards, development paradigms, and what counts as innovation. *We must question who sets the agenda, who benefits from it, and what values are embedded in the tools we export.*

There are alternatives. Legal AI need not be imperial. Participatory co-design, open-source models, and culturally responsive algorithms offer a different path. In Colombia, a civic tech initiative trained community paralegals to use natural language processing tools adapted to local Spanish dialects. In Ghana, NGOs partnered with local software engineers to build dispute resolution platforms that recognise both statutory and customary outcomes. In Indonesia, hybrid court models combine human mediation with digital scheduling, preserving the ritual elements of justice while easing administrative burdens. These examples prove that legal innovation can *enhance local sovereignty, not erode it.*

But doing so requires a fundamental shift in mindset. Exporting legal technology must be reframed not as a civilising mission, but as a cross-cultural dialogue. Development agencies and multinational firms must move beyond compliance checklists and adopt principles of *technological humility*. This means recognising that legal systems are not problems to be solved, but traditions to be engaged. That algorithms are not neutral, but normative. That modernisation is not synonymous with Westernisation.

If the future of law is increasingly algorithmic, then global justice demands more than universal standards. It demands contextual intelligence, local authorship, and epistemic respect. The challenge is not just to transfer tools—but to co-create systems that reflect the aspirations, pluralities, and dignity of the communities they serve. Anything less risks repeating the mistakes of the past, now encoded in lines of code. And in doing so, it reaffirms what this chapter's title names plainly: *global inequality, by design.*

A New Social Contract for Legal AI

In 1762, Jean-Jacques Rousseau asked what makes authority legitimate. His answer—*the general will* expressed through the social contract—became a cornerstone of democratic theory. Centuries later, the rise of artificial intelligence in law demands we revisit the same question: *What authorises decisions when they are made by machines, coded by private actors, and deployed without consent?* The legal profession, once bound by oaths, constitutional mandates, and democratic checks, now shares terrain with systems that operate invisibly, impersonally, and without recourse. As algorithmic power grows, so too must our frameworks for legitimate governance. A new social contract is overdue—not between citizens and the state, but between society and its increasingly digital instruments of justice.

Artificial intelligence is not just another tool added to the lawyer's desk. In many contexts, it has begun to replace or obscure the human processes of judgment, discretion, and accountability that underpin the rule of law. Legal AI now drafts contracts, predicts recidivism, adjudicates benefits, and even recommends sentencing—all while operating behind proprietary firewalls and with limited public oversight. When such systems become infrastructural—essential, ubiquitous, and unregulated—they no longer merely assist the law; *they start to become it.* The moral urgency here is not to halt innovation, but to re-centre legitimacy as a precondition for technological integration.

Consent is the first casualty in this transformation. Citizens rarely know when AI is used in legal processes that affect them, let alone how it works or on what grounds its recommendations rest. In the United Kingdom, the use of facial recognition technologies by police forces proceeded for years without statutory basis or parliamentary debate. In the United States, risk assessment tools such as COMPAS were implemented in sentencing decisions despite opaque algorithms and demonstrable racial bias. Across jurisdictions, software makes life-changing decisions under the guise of objectivity, while the individuals affected have no meaningful opportunity to understand, contest, or opt out. *This is governance without consent, and it is antithetical to democratic ideals.*

Equally concerning is the *collapse of accountability.* Traditional legal actors—judges, lawmakers, barristers—are constrained by ethical duties, transparency obligations, and judicial review. AI systems are not. When a system misclassifies a tenant for eviction, or erroneously denies a benefit, it is unclear who is responsible: the vendor? the programmer? the public agency that adopted the system? Legal doctrines of liability lag behind the complexity of distributed technological decision-making. This is no longer a theoretical issue. In the Netherlands, the SyRI algorithm used to detect welfare fraud was found to violate human rights, yet no individual or institution was held liable. *Without accountability, harm becomes procedural error—regrettable but unredressable.*

What, then, would a social contract for legal AI look like? At minimum, it must rest on *three pillars*: legitimacy, consent, and accountability. Legitimacy requires that systems used in legal decision-making be authorised by democratically enacted laws, not silently procured through administrative convenience. Consent demands that individuals have the right to know when automated systems are used, and the ability to meaningfully challenge their outcomes. Accountability entails that decisions made or shaped by AI must be traceable, reviewable, and governed by enforceable standards of fairness and due process.

This is not a matter of ethics alone. It is a matter of public law. Just as constitutions constrain the power of legislatures and executives, so too must legal frameworks constrain the deployment of algorithmic authority. Yet too often, governments adopt legal tech before they regulate it, lured by promises of efficiency, cost reduction, and innovation. These priorities are understandable—but they are not neutral. When convenience trumps legitimacy, the public loses its role in shaping how justice is defined and delivered.

One proposed model is the *Algorithmic Impact Assessment (AIA)*—a procedural mechanism that requires government agencies to disclose and evaluate the potential effects of automated decision systems before implementation. Pioneered in Canada and debated in the European Union, AIAs draw inspiration from environmental and human rights impact assessments, placing the burden on public bodies to justify technological adoption. While promising, AIAs remain advisory in most jurisdictions, lacking teeth and enforceability. For a genuine social contract, such assessments must become legally binding and subject to judicial review.

Transparency, though essential, is insufficient on its own. Open-source code may improve scrutiny, but it does not guarantee understanding or redress. The more critical move is to embed *contestability* into legal AI—designing systems with the assumption that their decisions will be challenged, and that those challenges must be heard by humans who understand the technology and the law. This is not a technical feature—it is a democratic right. *A justice system in which decisions cannot be questioned is not a justice system at all.*

Critics argue that legal AI cannot be governed in this way without stifling innovation. But this frames regulation as a brake rather than a compass. The better view is that legitimacy itself is a condition for sustainable innovation. Just as medical technologies require ethical trials, and financial systems demand regulatory approval, legal technologies must prove themselves in the crucible of democratic scrutiny. A market-led approach cannot substitute for public legitimacy. The stakes are too high.

Examples of this principle in practice are beginning to emerge. In New Zealand, proposed laws require that any automated system used in the administration of public decisions be publicly registered and subject to auditing. In France, the use of predictive analytics in judicial decision-making has been limited by statute, reaffirming the primacy of judicial reasoning. In Brazil, data protection laws explicitly recognise algorithmic bias as a violation of individual rights. These initiatives are nascent, uneven, and politically contested—but they mark the outlines of a future in which legal AI is governed as a public institution, not a private convenience.

The notion of a social contract implies mutual obligation. It demands that those who wield power—be they governments or companies—do so under conditions that the public can recognise as fair, reasonable, and justifiable. For legal AI, this means recognising that *code is not neutral, and deployment is not consent.* It means moving beyond ethics panels and glossy white papers, toward enforceable norms backed by democratic processes. It means ensuring that every person affected by algorithmic decision-making retains the right to be heard, to be understood, and to be treated as more than a data point.

As we reimagine the legal profession in the algorithmic age, we must also reimagine the structures that legitimise it. The law is not a software service. It is a collective expression of values, history, and negotiated commitments. When AI enters that domain, it must do so as a servant—not a sovereign. The new social contract must remind us that technology is never just technical. It is a choice. And justice, ultimately, is a relationship: between institutions and people, rules and reasons, authority and accountability. That relationship must be reaffirmed—digitally, deliberately, and democratically.

Chapter 9
What Should Never Be Automated

There are questions that no algorithm ought to answer. Not because it lacks capability, but because doing so would deform the very nature of the question, which demands judgment, conscience, and human accountability. As artificial intelligence extends its reach—from traffic citations to contract enforcement—the temptation grows to entrust it with far weightier matters: asylum decisions, child custody, parole hearings. Yet there is a profound distinction between streamlining bureaucracy and outsourcing moral responsibility. When code substitutes for conscience, it is not merely performing a function; it is assuming a duty it cannot bear. The challenge, then, is not to perfect the machinery, but to draw a boundary. Not everything that can be automated should be.

This chapter confronts the threshold question that technocratic enthusiasm tends to skirt: where must automation be refused—not from fear, but principle? Answering this requires more than engineering caution or procedural guidance; it demands philosophical clarity. There is a critical difference between tasks that are complicated and those that are complex—between procedures that can be formalised and ethical decisions that implicate dignity, autonomy, and the irreducible plurality of human lives. As legal philosopher Michael Sandel observes in other contexts, treating certain goods as commodities can corrupt their essence; the same applies to human judgement. Deploying automated decision-making in sensitive legal arenas risks more than error—it risks misunderstanding what justice itself entails.

Automation's appeal is seductive: faster, cheaper, more consistent. Yet law, at its core, is not a production line—it is a cultural and moral institution charged with interpreting meaning amid ambiguity. Consider the contrast between processing a tax refund and adjudicating an asylum claim. The former is transactional, guided by clear eligibility rules; the latter is existential, rooted in unprovable narratives, trauma-laden testimony, and cross-cultural interpretation. Reducing such human experiences to data points—however sophisticated the algorithm—distorts what is being judged. Information is not understanding.

Even when AI achieves statistical parity with human actors, it may fail where it matters most. A predictive sentencing tool can calculate recidivism risk with empirical precision, yet it cannot perceive remorse, gauge intent, or assess transformation—the subtleties a judge must consider. The law must evaluate not merely actions, but persons. That capacity—grounded in mutual recognition, ethical imagination, and the willingness to bear the weight of fallibility—cannot be encoded. The gravest legal decisions—separating children from parents, granting asylum, imposing prison sentences—rely precisely on empathy, moral discernment, and the courage to decide in uncertainty.

Some argue that machines remove human bias and thereby enhance fairness. Partly true, yet partial understanding conceals a deeper problem. Human judges can be held accountable, appealed, corrected; machines—especially proprietary ones—may operate beyond scrutiny, protected by trade secrets and embedded in systems no single person can fully comprehend. The harm here is subtle, insidious, and insistent, clothed in a veneer of objectivity. The question is not whether humans err—we do—but whether we accept decisions that no human ultimately stands behind.

The urgency is most acute in family law and asylum proceedings, where legal determinations are inseparable from moral nuance and human vulnerability. In 2020, a child welfare algorithm in Allegheny County, Pennsylvania, disproportionately flagged poor and minority families for investigation. Intended to allocate services efficiently, it mirrored systemic inequities, turning surveillance into a self-reinforcing loop. In the UK, automated systems piloted for immigration screening raised concerns over racial profiling and wrongful rejections. These are not peripheral cases; they are sites where law confronts human fragility, and where errors leave scars beyond procedural remedy.

Preserving the integrity of legal judgment requires asserting why certain decisions must remain human. Extending John Rawls' "veil of ignorance," one might ask: would we accept a machine deciding our own asylum claim, divorce, or criminal sentence? If the answer is no, then we cannot ethically impose such mechanisms on those least able to resist. Legitimacy is tested not by convenience, but by reversibility: can we accept for ourselves what we impose on others?

This is not a repudiation of legal AI; it is a call for discernment. Automation has a proper domain: compliance checks, document triage, regulatory matching, routine case management. These applications improve access, reduce delay, and free human expertise for decisions that demand it. But tools are not judges. The danger is not merely that machines err, but that we forget what errors truly matter—a delayed filing is inconvenience; a child placed with the wrong caregiver is moral injury.

Thus, the critical question is not "Can AI do this?" but "Should we allow it?" Answering demands legal ethics and democratic debate, not technical confidence alone. Like medicine distinguishing between routine and complex care, law must identify domains where human deliberation is indispensable, where presence, not process, makes the difference. This requires scaffolding: clearly defined exclusion zones, mandated human oversight, public justification for adoption, and robust safeguards against abdication.

Drawing such lines is not a rejection of progress—it is its moral framing. We automate to enhance justice, not supplant it. That distinction demands discipline, humility, and above all, fidelity to the human beings at the heart of legal decisions. Law cannot be reduced to logic trees or probability scores without losing its essence. Forgetting this risks building systems that are fast, scalable, and utterly illegitimate. The task is not merely to build better tools, but to remember why justice exists—and to whom it must answer.

Drawing the Line

Not all progress is neutral. The diffusion of artificial intelligence into legal systems carries with it a gravitational pull—a momentum that makes it harder to say "no" as each technical success becomes justification for the next domain. Tax processing is automated; why not parking violations? Parking violations are automated; why not immigration appeals? The rationale slides from efficiency to inevitability. What begins as a tool for support threatens to become a proxy for decision-making. And so the question becomes urgent, not just technical: *Where should we draw the line?*

The law is not one monolithic practice but a constellation of functions—some rigid and rule-based, others fluid and interpretive. It is precisely because of this diversity that we must distinguish between domains where automation enhances the legal process and those where it degrades it. *There are areas of law where computation can—and should—do the heavy lifting. But there are others where the moral texture of the case cannot be flattened without ethical loss.* Making that distinction requires more than legal expertise; it demands conceptual clarity about what kind of reasoning the law requires in different contexts.

Consider the domain of regulatory compliance. Legal obligations tied to clearly defined triggers—reporting requirements, filing deadlines, statutory thresholds—lend themselves to automation because their logic is explicit, repeatable, and minimally contextual. In such domains, AI-powered systems can significantly reduce clerical burden, accelerate administrative throughput, and reduce human error. Compliance software in environmental law, for instance, can automatically flag violations based on sensor data and regulatory codes. No judgment is needed to know that emission levels exceeded permissible limits on a specific date. *When legal duties are transactional, automation can be liberating.*

Contract law offers another instructive case. For standardised commercial agreements—NDAs, leases, vendor contracts—automated drafting tools can produce usable documents in seconds, backed by well-tested templates. When the aim is consistency, speed, and reduction of routine labour, the gains are hard to dispute. Indeed, in high-volume legal operations—insurance claims, patent filings, company formation—automation does not replace legal reasoning so much as extend its reach, making access to basic legal functions cheaper and more widely available.

But the limits of automation become evident as soon as the law shifts from *what* happened to *why*, or from *did a rule apply* to *what ought the outcome to be*. These are the regions where judgment cannot be distilled into criteria. Take sentencing. While predictive algorithms such as COMPAS have been deployed in U.S. criminal courts to estimate recidivism risk, their use has drawn criticism for opacity, embedded bias, and the illusion of objectivity. An algorithm might estimate that a young man from a particular neighbourhood is statistically more likely to reoffend—but it cannot weigh his remorse, his aspirations, or the meaning of mercy in his case. *The moment law becomes interpretive, AI's claim to competence becomes ethically fragile.*

This is especially true in fields that implicate identity, trauma, or contested moral values. Family law is a canonical example. Deciding custody is not a matter of applying rules to facts—it is about envisioning a future in which a child's emotional, psychological, and developmental needs are nurtured. No algorithm can meaningfully model the quality of maternal affection or the risks of domestic volatility. To try is to mistake human vulnerability for data. Similarly, in asylum law, where an individual's fate may rest on how convincingly they recount their fear of persecution, decision-making must account for trauma, translation, and cultural expression. A uniform standard applied by machines may ensure consistency—but at the cost of fairness.

It is tempting to counter that humans, too, are inconsistent, biased, or emotionally driven in ways that undermine ideal judgment. This is true. But it misses a crucial difference. Human judges *can be challenged*, their reasoning scrutinised, their biases debated in public. Algorithms, particularly proprietary ones, often operate as black boxes—deciding without explaining, shaping outcomes with no visible lines of accountability. *To accept a machine's decision without recourse to reasons is not merely bad jurisprudence—it is undemocratic.* Consent to be ruled includes the right to understand and contest how rulings are made.

The stakes are not only institutional but moral. Law functions not merely as a mechanism for order but as a forum for recognition. It is the space where society signals what matters, what counts as harm, and who deserves redress. When a judge listens to testimony in a courtroom, they are not just assessing claims—they are witnessing, affirming that the claimant's story exists in the moral imagination of the polity. Delegating such moments to automated systems risks erasing this recognition. It reduces the citizen to a data profile and the law to a sorting algorithm.

Drawing the line, then, is less about delineating domains of technical feasibility than articulating domains of ethical necessity. One way to frame this is by asking whether the legal task in question requires empathy, contextual reasoning, or normative discretion. If it does, it should not be automated. Tax calculation? Automate. Bail decisions? Require human oversight. Document discovery? Automate. Deportation rulings? Human, always. These are not merely practical distinctions—they are assertions about where moral agency belongs.

There is also a danger in the middle ground, where hybrid systems—part human, part machine—create the illusion of oversight without genuine accountability. A judge who mechanically adopts a risk score without questioning its premises is no more autonomous than the algorithm they rely on. The challenge is to ensure that humans remain responsible *and* empowered to act independently of machine recommendations. That requires more than user interfaces; it requires legal doctrine and institutional design that protect human authority, not just preserve its appearance.

One promising direction is to codify what might be called "zones of human obligation"—categories of legal decisions that, by their very nature, demand human authorship. Just as some jurisdictions prohibit mandatory sentencing guidelines in favour of judicial discretion, legal systems could define protected domains where automation is either restricted or explicitly subordinated to human judgment. Another approach is to mandate explainability—not only of machine outcomes but of their underlying assumptions and limitations. *Transparency is not a technical feature but a political right.*

Ultimately, drawing the line is about more than risk management. It is a statement about what kind of society we want to be. A society that automates everything it can is not necessarily more advanced—it is merely more efficient. A just society, by contrast, is one that *chooses not to automate certain things because it understands their human significance.* That choice requires discernment, not dogma; democratic engagement, not blind adoption; legal innovation that respects the boundary between utility and meaning.

To navigate this terrain, lawyers, technologists, and policymakers must cultivate a new kind of literacy—one that blends legal reasoning with ethical foresight and a willingness to ask: *What are we willing to hand over, and what must we always keep?* That is not a question for coders alone. It is a constitutional question in the broadest sense—a test of whether the machinery of justice still belongs to the people it claims to serve. Drawing the line is not a failure of imagination. It is an act of civic courage.

The Moral Limits of Machine Judgment

A machine can score a loan application in seconds, generate contract language with astonishing precision, and predict recidivism rates with alarming confidence. Yet no matter how efficient or statistically accurate such systems become, there remains a realm of human judgment they cannot—and arguably must not—enter. It is in this domain, where dignity, moral responsibility, and the burden of conscience reside, that the very limits of machine judgment reveal themselves. For all the promise of AI in legal systems, it is precisely *what cannot be automated* that deserves our most careful attention.

At the heart of modern jurisprudence lies the irreducible fact that justice is not merely a calculation. It is a moral activity: it demands interpretation, empathy, deliberation, and the capacity to account for context that resists abstraction. As political philosopher Michael Sandel argues, justice is inextricably bound to notions of the good life—a subject on which societies have long disagreed. Similarly, John Rawls' idea of justice as fairness depends on the premise that individuals must reason from behind a "veil of ignorance," imagining rules as if they did not know their place in society. These are acts of moral imagination, not algorithmic computation. To delegate such reasoning to systems that lack sentience is not to delegate the task—it is to erase it.

Proponents of legal automation often argue that algorithms are more consistent than human judges, less prone to bias, and capable of processing complex patterns that human reasoning cannot. Yet this formulation rests on a dangerous assumption: that fairness is equivalent to uniformity, and that predictability is a proxy for justice. It is not. Consistency without conscience is not neutrality—it is indifference dressed up in precision. The law does not merely apply rules; it interprets them through the lens of human experience. To decide is to assume responsibility—not just for outcomes, but for the reasoning behind them.

Nowhere is this more evident than in emotionally charged legal domains such as family law or asylum adjudication. In custody battles, judges weigh not only legal precedent, but the unquantifiable needs of a child—the emotional texture of relationships, the credibility of lived experience, the prospect of future harm that defies modelling. In asylum decisions, officials must evaluate trauma, fear, persecution, and cultural nuance, all of which unfold in testimonies that are fragmented, painful, and profoundly human. To imagine that such assessments can be distilled into risk scores or confidence intervals is not only naive—it is ethically reckless.

Consider the example of the United States' COMPAS system, a risk assessment tool used in sentencing decisions. Although it was introduced to standardise bail and parole outcomes, studies revealed that the algorithm disproportionately flagged Black defendants as higher risk, even when controlling for prior records. The company behind COMPAS, Northpointe (now Equivant), refused to disclose its proprietary formula, citing trade secrecy. What followed was not just a debate about accuracy, but about legitimacy. *When the rules that govern liberty and punishment are hidden in code, the very idea of justice becomes opaque.*

This is not a technical flaw—it is a philosophical crisis. For a society governed by law to be just, its processes must be not only efficient, but intelligible and contestable. A machine that cannot explain its reasoning cannot be held accountable. Worse, it cannot be asked to reflect, to regret, or to change. The very faculties that make human judgment fallible—empathy, doubt, moral anguish—are the same ones that make it *responsible.* In stripping judgment of these traits, we risk stripping justice of its humanity.

Rawls' theory of public reason insists that legitimate laws must be justifiable to all citizens, regardless of their worldview. This requires that the grounds of legal decisions be shared, scrutinised, and debated in public. Proprietary AI systems short-circuit this democratic condition by substituting private optimisation goals—such as cost reduction or throughput—for public values like equity and deliberation. As these systems increasingly inform legal decisions, we must ask: *who are they optimised for, and who is excluded from their logic?*

Michael Sandel warns against the moral hollowing that occurs when markets invade spheres once governed by ethical norms. Something similar is happening with legal automation: we risk turning ethical deliberation into a service metric, and replacing principled disagreement with statistical smoothing. Justice, like democracy, thrives not on agreement but on legitimate conflict—on the capacity to argue, to object, to reason together. Algorithms trained on historical data, however, replicate patterns. They do not challenge them. They can perpetuate injustice with the imprimatur of objectivity.

One might argue that systems can be designed to incorporate fairness metrics, transparency protocols, or post-decision audits. These are necessary safeguards—but they do not solve the core problem. *Judgment is not an output; it is an act.* To judge is to be morally exposed, to stand behind a decision, and to acknowledge that another person's life may be irrevocably altered by your reasoning. No machine, no matter how advanced, bears that burden. It can simulate choices, but it cannot *choose* in the ethical sense. It does not have to live with its decision.

This distinction matters because law is not simply a coordination system—it is a moral architecture. It encodes our collective aspirations, protects the vulnerable, disciplines power, and makes space for mercy. The automation of legal processes cannot be approached as a mere technical upgrade. It is a transformation of institutional logic. And if it proceeds unchecked, we risk replacing the deliberative foundations of justice with the procedural regularities of a black box.

This does not mean that all forms of legal AI are inherently illegitimate. Document review, statutory search, contract drafting—these are domains where automation can reduce drudgery and enhance efficiency without usurping moral agency. But we must draw a firm line between tools that support human judgment and systems that attempt to replace it. That line is not technical—it is ethical. It must be drawn with clarity, courage, and humility.

Ultimately, what is at stake is not whether machines can think like humans, but whether we are willing to abandon the moral responsibility that comes with human judgment. The pressure to automate—to render everything measurable, mappable, and optimisable—must be resisted where it threatens the very conditions of justice: dignity, responsibility, conscience, and care. In those domains, we must reclaim not only the right to judge, but the duty to do so.

Justice without judgment is not justice. It is procedure without principle, efficiency without empathy, and decision without responsibility. In the age of machine reasoning, preserving the moral limits of judgment is not a technological constraint—it is a human imperative.

Case Study: AI in Family Law and Asylum

The line between decision support and decision displacement is never more perilous than in domains where lives can be shattered by a single bureaucratic error. In family law and asylum adjudication, the stakes are existential, the narratives are tangled, and the consequences of misjudgement can be lifelong and irreversible. These are not merely legal questions—they are moral tests of how a society treats the vulnerable. Yet these very spaces, dense with ambiguity, emotion, and cultural complexity, are now being targeted by AI-driven tools promising efficiency, consistency, and cost reduction. That promise, when transplanted into contexts of such human fragility, becomes a threat.

Family law cases routinely navigate issues of abuse, parental alienation, trauma, addiction, financial hardship, and child welfare—often simultaneously. The assessment of a child's best interest is not a rule-following exercise; it is a deeply interpretive act that relies on testimony, emotion, historical relationships, and a forward-looking sense of what stability and safety might look like. When courts introduce algorithmic tools into this terrain—tools that rank risk, flag inconsistencies, or prioritise certain factors in custody decisions—they risk enshrining partial perspectives into systems that masquerade as objective.

Take, for instance, the increasing use of risk assessment algorithms in child protective services. In Allegheny County, Pennsylvania, a predictive risk model is used to score child welfare referrals. Drawing from vast troves of public data—welfare records, criminal histories, school attendance—the system generates a numerical score that influences whether a human caseworker investigates. Independent audits of the model revealed racial disparities: calls involving Black children received higher risk scores even when the underlying facts were comparable to those for white children. Here, the veneer of algorithmic neutrality cloaked structural inequalities, amplifying them under the guise of diligence.

Family law is already fraught with unequal access to representation, cultural misunderstandings, and judicial discretion coloured by unconscious bias. Adding algorithmic systems that inherit the same biases, encode them, and then deploy them at scale does not level the playing field—it buries the unevenness deeper beneath layers of computation. Worse, these systems often operate with limited transparency. A parent denied custody because of an opaque risk score may never know what data was used or how it was weighted. The right to be heard becomes procedural rather than substantive—satisfied by a process that listens to data but not to people.

In asylum law, the dangers intensify. Seeking asylum is not an administrative task; it is a plea for protection often made in desperation, by individuals fleeing war, persecution, torture, or death. The 1951 Refugee Convention requires that claims be considered individually and fairly, with recognition of the complex, deeply personal factors that inform fear and credibility. Yet in countries like the United States and the United Kingdom, asylum decision-making is increasingly supplemented or supplanted—by digital tools. These range from language analytics that assess credibility based on consistency, to automated forms that categorise applicants according to threat level or likelihood of approval.

One such tool, the Canadian Immigration and Refugee Board's "Chinook" system, was designed to streamline visa processing by allowing officers to review multiple applications in bulk with pre-populated data fields. Critics argue that Chinook, far from merely aiding decisions, creates cognitive blinders—encouraging officers to focus on risk indicators extracted by algorithm while sidelining individual narratives. Decisions that should be slow, deliberative, and attuned to nuance are instead nudged toward speed and scale. *This is not a question of assistance; it is a question of who frames what counts as relevant.*

In 2020, an AI system deployed by the Dutch tax authority to detect child benefit fraud falsely flagged over 20,000 families—many of immigrant background—as fraudulent, based on a flawed algorithm that assigned disproportionate risk to dual-nationality households. The human cost was staggering: families lost access to childcare, livelihoods were ruined, and psychological trauma ran deep. Though not an asylum case, the scandal illustrates how machine judgment in sensitive bureaucratic contexts can cause systemic harm when driven by optimisation imperatives divorced from human accountability.

The underlying logic of many AI systems—pattern recognition from historical data—becomes ethically perverse in asylum cases. By definition, persecution is often exceptional; trauma does not conform to patterns; and the credibility of a refugee's account may hinge on cultural factors that resist translation into quantifiable indicators. If an algorithm learns from past approvals, it may begin to standardise the very forms of testimony that sound familiar to Western ears, penalising those whose experiences fall outside its training set. This is not just misrepresentation—it is moral erasure.

The problem is compounded by the black-box nature of many AI systems. Refugees, often with limited legal representation, cannot meaningfully challenge the decisions made against them if the logic behind those decisions is hidden behind proprietary code. A process that should embody procedural justice instead becomes Kafkaesque—opaque, unaccountable, and immune to redress.

Defenders of these systems point to resource constraints. Courts are overloaded; immigration systems are backlogged; child welfare services are underfunded. Technology, they argue, is not a panacea but a triage tool—necessary for managing overwhelming caseloads. But necessity does not negate ethical scrutiny. *A tool that helps manage workload but increases the likelihood of injustice is not a neutral tool; it is a policy choice cloaked in code.*

There is also a deeper philosophical tension. Family law and asylum adjudication require more than just rule application—they require *judgement.* That is, the capacity to navigate moral grey zones, to hear pain, to discern credibility, and to adapt principle to circumstance. Machines can replicate form but not substance; they can process data but not meaning. These domains call for not just legal knowledge but emotional intelligence, cultural literacy, and the courage to weigh consequences that cannot be quantified. Automating these faculties is not just risky—it is an abdication of moral responsibility.

What would responsible AI look like in these contexts? It would begin not with the drive to replace judgment, but to support it. A well-designed system could surface inconsistencies to prompt closer human scrutiny—not act as an oracle. It could flag outlier patterns while preserving discretion. Crucially, it would be *auditable*—subject to challenge, explanation, and revision. It would operate under the assumption that human dignity requires not just accurate outcomes, but *meaningful process.*

Such systems would also be co-designed with those affected. Refugee advocates, social workers, family lawyers, and marginalised communities must have a voice in shaping the systems that govern them. Technical expertise is necessary, but insufficient. The legitimacy of a legal system rests not only on what it delivers, but on how—and for whom—it makes decisions.

Finally, we must reject the notion that emotion contaminates legal reasoning. In family law and asylum, emotional insight is not bias—it is *sensitivity to human complexity*. A legal system that seeks to sterilise emotion in the name of consistency risks producing not fairness but cruelty. *Compassion is not the opposite of objectivity; it is the condition of responsible judgment where lives are at stake.*

If we treat family law and asylum as testbeds for automation, we normalise the idea that ethical complexity is just another inefficiency to be optimised away. But if we hold the line here—if we insist that these domains remain rooted in human judgment, transparency, and deliberative care—then we model a better standard for how legal AI can serve rather than supplant justice. Not every domain can tolerate shortcuts. Some require the long, slow work of listening, reflecting, and deciding in full view of the human stakes. Those are the domains where our humanity is revealed—not only in what we decide, but in how we choose to decide at all.

Guardrails for the Future

The most dangerous technologies are not those that malfunction—they are the ones that function precisely as designed, while we remain unprepared for their consequences. Legal AI falls squarely in this category. Deployed in courts, regulatory agencies, immigration systems, and law enforcement, these systems are not on the periphery of governance. They are assuming core functions of judgment, discretion, and interpretation—without the epistemic humility, procedural transparency, or moral accountability that these tasks demand. The question is no longer whether AI should assist in legal decision-making. The imperative now is to draw principled boundaries—*to articulate where it can help, where it must be checked, and where it must be categorically excluded.*

The challenge, however, lies in defining criteria that go beyond vague appeals to "ethics" or "fairness." Platitudes won't suffice. Policymakers, technologists, and citizens alike need a framework—one rooted in legal theory, democratic legitimacy, and practical governance—that can guide decision-making across contexts. The urgency is not hypothetical. From facial recognition tools in policing to proprietary sentencing algorithms, from refugee screening systems to tax audit flagging mechanisms, we are already witnessing the delegation of high-stakes legal decisions to systems not designed for moral reasoning. The only thing missing is *intentional oversight.*

A responsible future requires a new grammar of governance—one that does not confuse speed with wisdom or data with justice. That grammar begins with three baseline commitments: *legitimacy, consent, and accountability.* Each offers a lens through which to assess whether and how legal AI should operate within a democratic society.

Legitimacy is the cornerstone. A legal decision, to be legitimate, must be grounded in a recognised legal authority, follow due process, and remain open to challenge. When AI systems are deployed without a legislative mandate, with unclear boundaries, or embedded within systems that lack public visibility, they erode the legitimacy of legal institutions. Consider the use of "predictive policing" tools in American cities. These systems, often developed by private vendors using proprietary data, claim to forecast where crimes are likely to occur. But their use has often bypassed legislative scrutiny, existing in a regulatory grey zone where police departments sign contracts without public input, courts defer to technical complexity, and citizens are left unaware of the surveillance shaping their neighbourhoods.

Consent adds another layer. In liberal democracies, legal authority derives not simply from efficiency but from the consent of the governed. People must know which systems are being used, how decisions are being made, and whether they have recourse to contest or opt out. Yet consent is notably absent in many AI-driven legal environments. Most defendants, asylum seekers, or litigants are never told that an algorithm influenced their case. Even lawyers and judges often do not understand how these systems function. *Opacity becomes the default*, not because secrecy is necessary, but because no one has required otherwise.

Then comes *accountability.* Who is responsible when an AI system gets it wrong—when a bail recommendation system leads to unwarranted detention, or a tax fraud flagging tool erroneously destroys a family's finances? Technologists point to the court. Courts defer to technical expertise. Vendors invoke trade secrets. *Accountability diffuses, and injustice multiplies.* Without enforceable accountability mechanisms—disclosure requirements, human oversight thresholds, legal liability regimes—these systems function without brakes.

So what might a meaningful framework look like? One that doesn't merely review code for bias but asks deeper questions about *institutional role*, *democratic process*, and *value pluralism*. The first step is **functional demarcation**—a recognition that not all legal decisions are equal in kind. We can distinguish between:

Administrative optimisation: tasks like filing deadlines, document routing, or notification systems—where automation may be safe, efficiency-enhancing, and ethically unproblematic.

Assisted analysis: using AI to surface relevant case law, flag inconsistencies in documentation, or suggest sentencing benchmarks—provided the human retains full discretion and understands the tool's limitations.

Partial delegation: where systems generate recommendations that carry presumptive weight unless actively overruled—a subtle but dangerous drift that can lead to automation bias.

Full delegation: where the machine renders the decision, and the human merely oversees implementation. This is where the guardrail must be hardest.

In legal domains involving *high moral density*—like asylum, parental rights, criminal sentencing, or constitutional adjudication—*full delegation should be off the table.* The logic here is not technological incapacity but moral non-substitutability. These decisions involve dignity, human suffering, and public trust in ways that exceed optimisation metrics. To automate them is not to improve process; it is to redefine what the legal system considers worth understanding.

Critically, any framework must include *mandatory transparency protocols.* Systems used in public governance must be open to independent audit—not only of their outputs, but of their training data, design assumptions, and embedded value hierarchies. Trade secrecy cannot be allowed to shield systems that exercise state power. Where full source code disclosure is impractical, robust third-party audit rights must be guaranteed by law.

Furthermore, the regulatory structure should mandate *explainability at the point of use.* Every individual subject to a legal decision influenced by AI should have the right to receive a meaningful explanation of how that decision was reached and what role the system played. This is not merely procedural courtesy; it is a condition of contestation, appeal, and human dignity.

To sustain this framework, we also need *institutional capacity*. Regulators must be trained not only in law but in computational thinking. Courts must develop technical literacy. Legislatures must be equipped to interrogate the social and ethical implications of AI systems. *Governance is not a byproduct of innovation; it is its precondition.*

And perhaps most crucially, we must reject the premise that legal AI is inevitable and therefore beyond control. This is a narrative often peddled by vendors and policymakers eager to appear forward-looking. But inevitability is not a principle—it is an abdication. Legal systems are not meant to follow technological trends. They are meant to shape them, channel them, and—when necessary—resist them. The fact that something is technically possible does not mean it is politically, morally, or legally justified.

That resistance must come not only from lawmakers but from civil society. Public participation in shaping the guardrails of legal AI is essential. This means more than consultative workshops or post hoc impact assessments. It means embedding deliberative democracy into the design phase of legal technologies. It means funding counter-expertise, ensuring plural voices are represented, and fostering public literacy so that AI in law is not something done *to* citizens, but something shaped *with* them.

Lastly, any credible framework must incorporate *sunset clauses* and *revision triggers*. AI systems deployed in law must not be treated as permanent fixtures. Their mandates should expire unless actively renewed after empirical evaluation. Their assumptions should be revisited regularly. Legal systems must be dynamic, not because technology evolves, but because *societies change*, *values shift*, and *harms accumulate* in ways that cannot always be foreseen.

A world in which AI quietly reconfigures the architecture of legal power is not science fiction—it is a policy failure. But that failure is not inevitable. With rigour, humility, and moral clarity, we can set the terms under which legal AI earns its place—or is denied it. The guardrails we build now will determine not only which tools we allow into our legal systems, but which values we protect from automation itself. That is the deeper question: not whether machines can perform legal tasks, but *what kind of legal order we are willing to entrust to them.* And what kind of human judgment we still believe should never be replaced.

Chapter 10
Designing for Judgment

Judgment is not a conclusion to be reached; it is a process—deliberative, provisional, interpretive, and accountable. It entails weighing competing values, anticipating unintended consequences, and accepting responsibility for the irreducible uncertainties of decision-making. Yet when legal technologists speak of "enhancing" judgment, they too often conflate it with prediction, precision, or optimisation. In that conflation lies a profound category error. Designing for judgment does not mean automating its outcomes; it means constructing conditions in which disagreement, accountability, and the possibility of repair remain structurally intact.

This chapter begins where most discussions of legal AI falter. It moves beyond transparency, explainability, and algorithmic fairness—not because these are unimportant, but because they are insufficient. A system may be transparent yet unaccountable; explainable yet incontestable; "fair" in code yet unjust in consequence. If legal AI is to support, rather than supplant, democratic institutions, its design must invite contestation. Systems must be built to be interrogated, challenged, revised, and appealed—not merely understood. The architecture of legal AI must mirror the political culture of law itself: pluralistic, adversarial, and procedurally open.

Contestability by design demands a rethinking of technical responsibility. Present approaches often treat "responsible AI" as post hoc correction: a flawed system is audited, biases patched, interfaces polished. But judgment cannot be retrofitted. If AI is to assist in morally charged areas—sentencing, asylum adjudication, benefits allocation—it must be designed from the outset to accommodate ambiguity, recognise dissent, and preserve space for human discretion. This is not a flaw to be fixed; it is the normative backbone of legality.

What, then, does it mean to build legal AI that supports judgment rather than simulating it? The answer begins with legal theory. Law is not a rulebook or database; it is a practice rooted in interpretation, reasoning, and adversarial exchange. Encoding legal reasoning into digital systems risks flattening this complexity into decision trees or probabilistic outputs—unless the system is intentionally designed to provoke interpretation. This means preserving audit trails, highlighting value-laden trade-offs, and enabling users—lawyers, judges, claimants—to contest conclusions meaningfully.

Consider algorithmic risk assessments in criminal justice. These tools, used in bail hearings, sentencing, and parole boards, often produce a numerical score based on historical data. Typically, that score is treated as definitive. Few systems clarify why an individual was deemed high- or low-risk, and fewer still allow the defendant to contest underlying assumptions or provide context. What emerges is not interpretability, but the erosion of interpretation: humans become rubber-stamps for algorithmic logic, not custodians of judgment.

Contrast this with a deliberative model. Imagine a sentencing support system that presents multiple interpretive framings, highlights uncertainties, flags legal thresholds, and surfaces past cases with divergent outcomes. Imagine further that it logs all human overrides, enabling courts to trace when and why the system's suggestions were rejected. Here, the focus shifts from automation to accountability: the machine provokes thought rather than substitutes for it.

Accountability by architecture requires recognising that every design decision is normative. Whether a system allows explanation or obscures it, prioritises efficiency or deliberation, logs dissent or suppresses it—these choices encode assumptions about law, whom it serves, and how disagreement is handled. Systems lacking traceability or metadata foreclose responsibility. Efficiency may be achieved, but governance is impossible.

By contrast, legal AI designed with interpretability layers, contestation hooks, and revision protocols invites democratic engagement. Litigants, advocates, and regulators can peer inside the black box—not just to understand outcomes, but to question them: Was this reasonable? Just? Should it stand? These are legal, not engineering, questions—and they can only be asked if the system is architected to receive them.

Even the best-designed systems rely on the institutions that govern them. Legal AI conversations have long been siloed between technologists and theorists. What is needed is institutional literacy: a practical understanding of how AI reshapes legal assumptions and power. Lawyers must grasp how probabilistic systems frame categories; technologists must understand how legal norms constrain discretion; citizens must know when an algorithm has affected their legal fate and how to contest it.

This is not a call for universal coding literacy, but for institutional sensibility—a recognition of how power circulates, responsibility is distributed, and norms are enforced. Judgment cannot be automated, but it can be supported. The challenge is to build systems that recognise the difference.

The legal system of the future will be hybrid—not because of technical inevitability, but democratic necessity. Neither humans nor machines alone can meet the demands of complex legal reasoning. Together, however, they can create an institutional configuration that respects the asymmetry of roles: machines process data, surface patterns, and flag anomalies; humans bear the burden of interpretation, responsibility, and justification. The aim is not to eliminate human error, but to preserve human judgment, informed by AI, not eclipsed by it.

Designing for judgment is not an abstraction; it is a political, legal, and design imperative. It requires resisting the allure of certainty in favour of systems that are corrigible, pluralistic, and contestable. Design is not interface decoration; it is institutional authorship. The measure of legal technology is not seamless integration, but how rigorously it preserves the conditions for disagreement. Only then can we call it legal. Only then can we call it just.

Beyond Transparency: Building for Contestation

Transparency has become the default virtue in the design of legal technologies. From regulatory white papers to ethics codes drafted by tech firms, there is a persistent assumption that rendering algorithmic systems "explainable" is sufficient to make them legitimate. The logic appears sound: if users can see how a decision was reached, they can assess its fairness. But in practice, transparency alone rarely delivers what it promises. An explanation is not a justification. A transparent process can still be inscrutable, arbitrary, or unjust. And perhaps more crucially, a system may explain itself perfectly and still leave no room to disagree with or revise its conclusions. *The heart of justice is not visibility—it is contestability.*

What distinguishes legal judgment from technical computation is not the ability to produce answers, but the capacity to interrogate them. Legal systems thrive on adversarial reasoning, on rights of appeal, on the possibility that even the most settled precedent can be challenged and overturned. These are not flaws to be debugged; they are *the moral scaffolding of law.* Yet too many algorithmic legal tools are designed as if legal reasoning were a linear function: input data, process with code, produce a decision. Once a result is outputted—be it a deportation order, a custody recommendation, or a risk score—it is treated as settled. The interface allows you to see the result. It rarely allows you to push back.

The distinction between transparency and contestability is more than semantic. It reflects fundamentally different theories of power. Transparency treats the user as a passive observer. It offers them a view inside the system's logic, but grants no authority to question its values or challenge its assumptions. Contestability, by contrast, treats the user as a rights-bearing agent. It acknowledges that in law, disagreement is not dysfunction—it is a feature. *To design for contestation is to institutionalise the possibility of dissent.*

Take, for instance, the COMPAS tool used in many US states to assist judges in bail and sentencing decisions. The tool calculates a defendant's "risk" of reoffending based on variables like age, criminal history, and employment status. The formula is proprietary, and the precise weightings are opaque even to the judges who rely on it. After public pressure, the creators released a general explanation of the variables used, but individual defendants still cannot interrogate how their specific score was derived. Nor can they meaningfully challenge the data used or the assumptions embedded in the model. *Transparency, such as it is, exists. Contestability does not.*

In a legal culture grounded in accountability, this is a democratic failure. The legitimacy of a court's decision rests not on its alignment with a dataset, but on the reasons it can give—reasons that others can contest, revise, or appeal. If legal technologies are to support rather than erode this legitimacy, they must be designed to preserve those conditions. This means systems must *surface the normative assumptions* on which they rest, *allow users to submit alternative evidence*, and *enable institutional actors to deviate from algorithmic suggestions*—and crucially, to do so with a recorded rationale.

Such design is not merely a technical exercise; it is an ethical and institutional commitment. It requires rethinking the architecture of AI systems not as engines of prediction, but as *provocations for deliberation.* Instead of treating AI outputs as endpoints, systems should present them as *tentative suggestions*, embedded in a context of pluralistic reasoning. A family law judge reviewing an AI-generated custody recommendation should not be nudged toward compliance by the tool's design. She should be encouraged to weigh it against other factors—some quantifiable, others irreducibly human. *The point is not to hide bias, but to allow contestable, contextualised judgment to prevail.*

To make this practical, legal AI systems must include certain features by design:

Interpretive traceability: Users must be able to follow how a decision was reached—not just in generic terms, but in case-specific logic. This goes beyond transparency and requires detailed audit trails, showing which data points influenced which intermediate conclusions.

Disagreement mechanisms: Systems must accommodate human override—not as an anomaly but as a normatively sanctioned act.

The interface should solicit dissent where appropriate, and document why a human decision-maker diverged from the AI's recommendation.

Input revision and new evidence: A truly contestable system must permit the submission of new data that can alter an outcome. This is particularly vital in dynamic legal contexts such as asylum law, where lived experience cannot be reduced to pre-set variables.

Appeal infrastructure: There must be clearly defined, legally enforceable pathways through which AI-generated decisions can be reviewed, appealed, and overturned—*not only within the system, but by independent oversight bodies.*

This design imperative runs counter to the prevailing ethos of efficiency in legal tech. It is slower, more costly, and less predictable. But it reflects a more honest understanding of what law is: a process that tolerates, and even requires, uncertainty and revision. A criminal sentencing algorithm that admits no meaningful challenge is efficient but illegitimate. A benefits algorithm that cannot be corrected by the claimant it affects is fast but unjust. *Speed is no substitute for dignity.*

There are already models emerging that point the way forward. In Canada, the use of AI tools in immigration adjudication was paused following widespread criticism over their opacity and inability to be challenged. The Canadian government responded with proposals requiring full disclosure of algorithms used in decision-making, and protocols for human review. In the Netherlands, the SyRI surveillance system—designed to detect welfare fraud through data mining—was struck down by a court for violating human rights norms, in part because its design left no room for individual contestation. *These are not just policy failures—they are design failures.*

To be clear, contestability does not mean that every decision must be debated endlessly. It means that decisions which significantly affect a person's rights or liberties must be subject to *structured opportunities for dissent.* In legal philosophy, this is sometimes called "procedural justice"—the idea that a fair process is as important as a correct outcome. People are more likely to accept a decision, even a painful one, if they feel they were heard, respected, and given the chance to contest it. *Legal AI must honour that procedural intuition, not bypass it.*

This is particularly important in high-stakes domains like asylum adjudication, child protection, or criminal justice, where decisions carry profound ethical weight. An AI system deciding refugee status cannot simply be transparent—it must allow the applicant to challenge its assumptions about credibility, risk, or intent. The applicant may not speak the system's language, may not fit its risk profile, may not have the type of data that the model considers "relevant"—but still, *they must be heard.* The system must be designed to accommodate such asymmetry, not erase it.

At its best, law is a site of structured contest. It is where we argue, revise, and repair—not because we mistrust reason, but because we acknowledge pluralism. No algorithm, however sophisticated, can capture the full moral texture of human judgment. But it can support it—*if it is built to be challenged.*

Designing for contestation is not an afterthought. It is not the next step after transparency. It is the condition that makes legal AI morally and politically viable. It means building systems that treat dissent not as a defect, but as a democratic necessity. It means designing for the moment when a human says, "No, that is not just," and having the system respond not with a blank screen, but with an invitation to revise. That is the true test of legitimacy—not whether an AI system can explain itself, but whether it can be *disagreed with.* Anything less is not legal reasoning. It is bureaucratic imposition masquerading as objectivity. And we should demand more.

Accountability by Architecture

A legal system's legitimacy does not rest merely on the laws it enforces, but on the structure by which it applies them. When algorithms are deployed to adjudicate rights, calculate penalties, or assign public benefits, their architecture becomes a source of political and ethical significance. Code is no longer just a tool—it is a procedural actor. The architecture of legal AI systems, down to how they record decisions, allow for appeals, or explain their reasoning, encodes values as much as any statute or precedent. Accountability, in this context, is not an afterthought. It is a design imperative.

What distinguishes legal institutions from private platforms or commercial software is not only their public function, but their constitutional commitments—due process, fairness, equal protection, and democratic oversight. An AI system that calculates bail eligibility or flags potential welfare fraud is not just automating efficiency; it is standing in the place of state authority. And yet, many of these systems are engineered without the procedural affordances that would make such authority answerable. *Design decisions become normative decisions.* What is logged, what is explainable, and what is revisable—these are not technical afterthoughts. They are architectural judgments about who gets to question power and on what terms.

Consider the design of audit trails. In traditional bureaucracies, documentation of decisions allows for appeal, oversight, and historical accountability. In digital systems, especially those driven by machine learning, the equivalent is the traceability of an algorithm's inputs and outputs—what data was used, what intermediate decisions were made, what weights and thresholds were applied. In some rule-based systems, this can be relatively straightforward. But in neural networks or systems incorporating probabilistic inference, the path from input to output may be difficult to reproduce, much less explain in natural language. Here, the architectural choice is stark: either design systems with interpretability layers that approximate the logic of decision-making, or accept opacity as a by-product of performance. Each path carries political weight.

Interpretability layers—such as decision visualisations, input influence maps, or proxy rule sets—can help bridge the gap between technical complexity and civic intelligibility. But too often, they are treated as optional extras. A legal AI system without a mechanism to explain its actions in terms comprehensible to its users is not just unaccountable—it undermines the very legitimacy of legal decision-making. When a litigant is denied parole, a refugee denied asylum, or a parent denied custody, it matters deeply whether they can understand why. *Explanation is not a courtesy. It is a democratic right.*

Transparency, however, is not synonymous with accountability. It is possible to reveal how a system works without giving users any ability to challenge its outcomes. Transparency shows the system. Accountability allows contestation. A well-designed system must include built-in affordances for dissent. This means more than merely offering a contact email or user feedback box. It means enabling appeals, logging contestations, allowing independent audits, and ensuring that those affected by a decision have a meaningful avenue for redress. An architecture of accountability embeds these features from the start, rather than retrofitting them after scandal.

This becomes especially critical in high-stakes domains. In the Netherlands, the SyRI scandal—a welfare fraud detection system—collapsed under constitutional scrutiny because it failed to provide adequate transparency or appeal to those it targeted. The system combined multiple databases to flag "risk" individuals, but offered neither clarity about its criteria nor opportunities to contest the label. Citizens were effectively black-boxed by their own government. The design failure here was not merely technical. It was a breakdown of democratic architecture: *an automated judgment without procedural remedy*.

Contrast this with Estonia's approach to digital governance, where systems are built with citizen-centric architecture. The Estonian Data Tracker, for example, allows citizens to see who has accessed their data, when, and for what purpose. This design decision—simple in theory, radical in its implications—reorients power. It turns the database into a site of reciprocal accountability. In legal AI, similar ideas are emerging: systems that log each decision point, flag anomalies for human review, or mandate justification codes for certain types of outcomes. These are not just features—they are *constitutional design elements*.

Yet much depends on institutional commitment. System design alone cannot guarantee democratic values if procurement policies, budget cycles, and oversight institutions do not prioritise them. Governments often purchase off-the-shelf AI tools without demanding interpretability or auditability. Procurement contracts that do not require meaningful accountability features implicitly normalise opacity. Design, in this sense, begins with the political imagination: *what do we ask for when we ask for legal AI?* A dashboard, or a defensible process?

There is also a critical distinction between front-end explanation and back-end justification. A system might provide surface-level user explanations—"Your application was denied due to incomplete documentation"—without exposing the deeper biases in its training data or decision rules. True accountability requires access to the system's assumptions. This is where architecture intersects with governance. Open standards, third-party audits, model documentation protocols like "datasheets for datasets" and "model cards" all represent attempts to move beyond mere disclosure toward structured scrutiny. But their uptake in the legal domain remains uneven.

Designing for accountability also involves anticipating institutional failure. What happens when a system goes wrong? Who is responsible? Can decisions be reversed, and how? These are not questions to be deferred until litigation. They are matters of architectural foresight. Version control, rollback protocols, decision provenance chains—these are features borrowed from robust software engineering, but they become juridically essential when applied to systems with legal authority. An architecture of accountability must be resilient to error, resistant to abuse, and responsive to contestation.

Critics may argue that building such robust systems is costly, and that public sector agencies lack the resources or expertise. But this is a false economy. The cost of unaccountable automation is not measured only in technical terms. It is measured in trust, legitimacy, and democratic coherence. The long-term damage of poorly designed legal AI—manifested in wrongful denials, opaque surveillance, or systemic bias—far outweighs the upfront investment required to build systems with procedural integrity. *Accountability is not a feature. It is the foundation.*

Finally, we must reject the idea that legal AI design is value-neutral. Choices about data sources, optimisation goals, error tolerances, and user interfaces all reflect normative assumptions. Are we optimising for efficiency, equity, or explainability? Are we minimising false positives or false negatives? Who gets to decide? Each of these decisions shapes the architecture in ways that affect the balance of power between state and citizen, judge and litigant, public and private actor. To design for accountability is to make those choices explicit, contestable, and subject to democratic revision.

The future of legal AI will not be decided by engineers alone. It will be built in the spaces where code meets constitution, where databases meet due process, and where design meets democratic theory. The systems we build today will set the procedural norms for a generation. Whether they support or subvert accountability depends not just on what they do, but on how they are built—and who gets to challenge them when they fail.

Institutional Literacy in the Age of AI

Modern legal systems are held together not only by statutes and courts, but by a deep, often invisible scaffold of assumptions—about how decisions are made, how discretion is exercised, and how citizens can hold institutions accountable. These assumptions are rarely taught explicitly, even to law students. They are absorbed through practice, culture, and precedent. Yet as artificial intelligence systems begin to mediate everything from tax enforcement to bail eligibility, those tacit norms are quietly rewritten. If AI is changing the operating logic of public institutions, then a new kind of literacy becomes essential—not just technical literacy, but institutional literacy: the ability to understand how systems work, what assumptions they encode, and how they shift the balance of power.

The introduction of AI into legal decision-making often masquerades as an efficiency upgrade. A system that triages visa applications faster or assigns judges more evenly may appear to enhance neutrality and throughput. But beneath that surface are structural reconfigurations. Who now holds discretion? What happens to appeal pathways? How does automation alter institutional memory or responsibility? These are not peripheral concerns. They cut to the heart of democratic legitimacy. Yet most citizens, professionals, and even some policymakers remain unequipped to interrogate these shifts—because they have not been taught how institutions function, let alone how AI might deform them.

Institutional literacy begins with understanding the foundational elements of legal process: the division between fact-finding and legal interpretation; the role of discretion in prosecutorial decisions; the principle of proportionality in sentencing; the mechanisms of appeal and review. These elements form the ethical skeleton of law—not because they guarantee justice, but because they enable contestation. They provide space for interpretation, dissent, and human judgment. When algorithmic systems are introduced into these spaces, they may preserve these features—or override them entirely. The question is whether users, professionals, and citizens can tell the difference.

Consider the example of COMPAS, the widely used risk assessment tool in American criminal justice. Judges use its scores to inform decisions on bail, parole, and sentencing. Yet the proprietary nature of the algorithm, combined with its opaque input criteria, makes it difficult even for trained professionals to evaluate its reasoning. A judge may receive a "high risk" score, but have little insight into which factors drove that determination—or how to question it. In this context, institutional literacy would mean knowing not just that a score was generated, but how such tools intersect with legal discretion, what constraints exist on their use, and how due process protections apply in AI-augmented environments.

This kind of understanding cannot be left to technologists alone. Legal professionals, civic educators, public administrators, and ordinary citizens all need tools to analyse how AI systems reshape institutional behaviour. What are the limits of automation in judicial contexts? How do feedback loops develop when predictive models influence policing patterns? What happens when citizens cannot contest algorithmic decisions that affect their rights? These are not engineering questions. They are questions of governance. And they demand education that blends legal reasoning with systems thinking.

At present, however, most legal education remains structurally detached from these issues. Law schools rarely teach students how digital systems are constructed, audited, or governed. Computer science departments, for their part, seldom offer serious instruction in public law, ethics, or institutional design. The result is a generation of lawyers who struggle to scrutinise algorithmic logic, and a generation of technologists who may lack the institutional imagination to anticipate legal consequences. This divide is no longer tenable. *Cross-disciplinary education is not optional—it is foundational.*

One promising model comes from the Public Interest Technology movement, which seeks to embed civic values into the design and deployment of emerging technologies. Programmes that pair law students with data scientists, or policy students with engineers, are beginning to surface in leading universities. But the scale is insufficient. To meet the moment, civic and professional education must be retooled across multiple fronts. Judges should be trained in algorithmic accountability. Journalists must learn how to interrogate data infrastructures. Civil society leaders need fluency in the logics of digital governance. And citizens, from high school onwards, should be taught how institutions function—not just formally, but dynamically—so that they can recognise when those functions are being silently rewritten by machines.

This is not a matter of technical literacy alone. Understanding how a machine learning model works does not tell you how it transforms procedural fairness. Conversely, knowing legal doctrine without recognising how digital systems codify or erode that doctrine leaves one blind to the true impact of automation. *Institutional literacy means seeing the whole terrain: how policy becomes code, how discretion is distributed, how accountability is structured.*

Take the case of the UK's Universal Credit system, an integrated welfare programme heavily reliant on algorithmic decision-making. Applicants must navigate a digital interface that automates many eligibility checks, payment calculations, and compliance monitoring. For those affected, the system often feels like a black box: delays occur without explanation, sanctions are applied automatically, and appeals become labyrinthine. The challenge here is not merely that the system is complex—it is that it departs from traditional welfare administration in ways that obscure responsibility. Who made the decision? Can it be appealed? Is the problem one of policy or implementation? Without institutional literacy, both users and advocates struggle to frame effective responses. *A citizen who does not know where to knock cannot ask for justice.*

Institutional literacy also matters for democratic participation. As governments increasingly adopt AI systems through procurement, public oversight depends on the ability of citizens and watchdogs to ask the right questions. Has the system been audited? Are there transparency obligations? What data was used in training, and is it representative? These are not abstract questions—they are the front lines of accountability. But they require more than curiosity. They require training.

One way forward is to integrate institutional analysis into digital literacy curricula at every educational level. This means teaching students not just how to code or use digital tools, but how public systems work—and how those systems are being reconfigured. What is an administrative hearing? How does a tribunal differ from a court? What is the role of evidence in judicial reasoning, and how might that role be altered by probabilistic scoring? By making these concepts accessible early on, we empower a generation of citizens to hold institutions to account—even when those institutions are mediated by software.

Another approach is to embed transparency and contestation rights directly into AI regulation. The EU's proposed AI Act, for example, requires that high-risk AI systems provide meaningful information to affected users, including logic, significance, and consequences of decisions. But regulatory provisions only go so far. To activate these rights, users must understand them. Here, education becomes enforcement. *A right not understood is a right not exercised.*

Professional associations also have a role to play. Bar associations, judicial colleges, civil service training bodies—all must update their curricula to reflect the realities of digital governance. This includes not just understanding specific tools, but the broader institutional shifts they represent: centralisation of decision authority, erosion of discretion, depersonalisation of interaction, and algorithmic bias. Training modules should move beyond compliance checklists to foster genuine reflection: when is automation appropriate? When is human oversight non-negotiable? What are the ethical thresholds we will not cross?

Critics may suggest that the speed of technological change outpaces the ability of institutions to adapt. But this is precisely why institutional literacy matters. It allows for principled adaptation, rather than reactive patchwork. It enables professionals to make informed decisions about when and how to incorporate AI into their workflows—and when to resist it. It equips citizens to demand that systems be not only efficient, but just. And it reminds us that even the most sophisticated technology cannot absolve us of the responsibility to understand, question, and shape the institutions that govern our lives.

AI is not replacing institutions. It is transforming them. Whether that transformation preserves democratic values or erodes them depends not just on the tools we build, but on the education we provide. Institutional literacy is not a luxury. It is the civic infrastructure of the digital age.

The Future Legal System is a Hybrid

A courtroom is not a spreadsheet. Law is not code. Yet the seduction of automation—of rules processed faster, decisions issued cheaper, disputes resolved "objectively"—continues to reshape the institutional imagination of legal systems worldwide. The core question is not whether artificial intelligence will be used in law; that is already a settled matter. From predictive policing to risk-scoring in parole decisions, algorithmic tools are already embedded within the machinery of justice. The critical question is how they should be used. The most dangerous illusion is that AI systems can replicate human judgment. The most responsible path forward is to design hybrid systems—legal infrastructures that integrate AI not to replace human decision-makers, but to support, refine, and rigorously challenge them.

There is a practical urgency to this vision. Courts in many jurisdictions are overwhelmed. Civil cases languish for years. Public defenders carry caseloads that defy comprehension. Governments face mounting pressure to deliver legal services efficiently, predictably, and at scale. AI promises relief: machine learning systems that can sort cases, summarise facts, even draft legal decisions. But when efficiency becomes the only metric of innovation, the foundations of justice begin to erode. A faster ruling is not necessarily a fairer one. An AI-generated judgment, however coherent, does not by itself confer legitimacy. *Justice depends not just on output, but on the process through which that output is reached.*

A hybrid legal system starts by recognising what machines are good at—and what they are not. AI excels at pattern recognition, data sorting, probabilistic estimation. It can rapidly detect inconsistencies across case law, surface relevant precedents, and flag anomalies in large datasets. These are valuable functions. In a hybrid system, AI can augment the analytical capabilities of judges, not supplant their reasoning. A well-designed system might provide a judge with a ranked list of applicable cases, flagging potential contradictions or latent biases in sentencing patterns. But the final interpretive move—the weighing of context, the exercise of conscience—remains with the human. *Interpretation is not a glitch in the legal process; it is the legal process.*

The distinction is not theoretical. In Estonia, a government pilot once proposed using AI to resolve small claims disputes under €7,000. While the system was never fully implemented, the idea was simple: feed both parties' submissions into an algorithm, let the system identify likely outcomes based on historical rulings, and issue a binding decision. The problem wasn't just one of accuracy. It was one of epistemic closure. A dispute resolved entirely by machine bypasses the performative and deliberative elements of law. The claimant never feels heard. The judge never sees the person behind the file. The system never pauses to ask whether this is a case that breaks the pattern. *In the rush to automate, we risk building a legal system that knows everything but understands nothing.*

Contrast this with the use of AI in legal research. Systems like ROSS Intelligence or Lexis+ AI already help lawyers extract relevant information from vast legal corpora. These tools can dramatically increase the speed and accuracy of research, especially for overburdened public defenders or under-resourced legal aid clinics.

Here, AI does not dictate outcomes; it enhances human capability. The tool is embedded within the practice of law, not imposed on top of it. This is what hybrid integration looks like: not substitution, but symbiosis.

But hybrid design also means building in friction—not as inefficiency, but as a safeguard. In aviation, autopilot systems are standard. Yet critical decisions still require a human pilot, and overrides are built into every control system. Legal AI should be no different. The goal is not blind deference, but *design for dissent.* Every AI-assisted decision in law must be challengeable. Every automated recommendation should include an interpretability layer that explains its reasoning in terms comprehensible to human decision-makers. Without such transparency, systems become unaccountable. Without contestability, they become authoritarian.

This demands an architectural shift. It is not enough to regulate outcomes; we must shape the structures that produce them. System design becomes a site of ethical decision-making. Will a case triaging system allow for manual override? Will a risk-scoring tool allow the subject to see and challenge their profile? Will automated contracts include mechanisms for renegotiation or human review in edge cases? *Accountability is not a feature to be retrofitted—it must be architected from the start.*

Hybrid systems also require new professional roles. Just as the rise of forensic science created specialised experts within the courtroom, so too will the rise of legal AI demand new intermediaries—algorithmic auditors, explainability officers, AI-literate advocates. These professionals will not merely translate between disciplines; they will uphold the boundary between technical feasibility and institutional legitimacy. Legal education must adapt accordingly. Tomorrow's lawyers will need to understand not only statutes and precedent, but how AI systems are trained, what data they ingest, and how they may encode bias. This is not a dilution of the profession. It is its renewal.

At the same time, the public must be brought into the design and oversight of hybrid legal systems. A model that serves only insiders will not retain legitimacy. Participatory governance—through citizen panels, oversight boards, or deliberative assemblies—can help determine where AI belongs, and where it must be excluded. Public values should inform system priorities. Should we optimise for speed, or for interpretive richness? Should certain domains—such as family law or asylum—be insulated from automation altogether? These are not engineering questions. They are civic ones. *Hybrid legal systems must remain democratic systems.*

This vision is not utopian. It is already taking root in various forms. In the Netherlands, the Hague Institute for Innovation of Law (HiiL) supports platforms that use AI to help citizens understand and navigate legal disputes, while preserving avenues for human mediation. In Canada, the British Columbia Civil Resolution Tribunal offers online dispute resolution with both automated tools and human oversight, ensuring that technology enhances access to justice without severing it from deliberative reasoning. In France, judicial data analytics systems are used internally to study case trends—not to automate decisions, but to improve institutional awareness. These examples illustrate the possibilities of hybrid design done well. The challenge is not inventing the model. It is scaling it responsibly.

There are, of course, tensions. Hybrid systems will never be fully neutral. They are shaped by priorities, resource constraints, and institutional culture. Embedding AI into law may entrench existing inequities if left unchecked. But the alternative—refusing AI altogether—risks irrelevance. Citizens increasingly expect public services to match the responsiveness of digital platforms. Legal systems that fail to evolve will lose public trust not because they are too slow, but because they seem out of step with reality.

The task, then, is to navigate between fatalism and fetishism. Fatalism says machines will take over legal judgment, whether we like it or not. Fetishism says we can build perfect tools if only we get the algorithms right. Both are wrong. The future of law will be neither fully automated nor wholly manual. It will be hybrid—if we design it that way. This means facing hard questions with intellectual honesty and civic imagination. Where does discretion matter most? When must a person—not a program—take responsibility? What design principles best preserve fairness, dignity, and accountability?

These are questions of governance, not gadgetry. They require not just innovation, but reflection. Not just code, but conscience. Not just machines that decide, but systems that deliberate. The legal systems of the future must blend speed with scrutiny, scale with specificity, logic with legitimacy. In short, they must be hybrid. Because the goal is not to make law more mechanical—it is to make it more human.

Chapter 11
The Burden of Knowing

Once it is perceived, it cannot be unseen. Such is both the peril and the insight of recognising how legal authority is increasingly mediated by code. At first glance, AI-assisted adjudication, predictive policing, algorithmic triage, and machine-generated verdicts may seem like instruments of efficiency—solutions to slow, inconsistent, or inaccessible justice. Yet the closer one looks, the more disorienting the view becomes. Law, even before AI, was never purely neutral; codification does not cleanse judgment—it reframes it. Automation, far from removing bias, often entrenches it behind walls of statistical legitimacy and corporate opacity. Understanding the system brings clarity, but also moral complexity. Once the reconstitution of power through code is visible, the question ceases to be whether action is required—it becomes how to respond responsibly.

This chapter begins at that critical juncture—after the data has been analysed, the models scrutinised, the cases considered. It confronts the reader not with answers, but with the weight of awareness. Consider a proprietary sentencing algorithm that can determine the length of a prison term, yet whose logic cannot be examined in court. Or the plight of refugee claimants whose cases are assessed partly by pattern-matching tools incapable of grasping trauma, context, or the nuances of fleeing persecution. These are not mere technical missteps. They are epistemic ruptures: fractures between the promise of due process and the reality of automated enforcement. Seeing the machine behind the curtain is not simply unsettling; it demands a moral and civic reorientation.

There is a tendency, particularly among well-intentioned reformers, to respond with calls for "better design": more transparent interfaces, improved datasets, refined models. Yet the argument here is more profound. It asks us to consider what we should never delegate—where human presence is indispensable. The challenge posed by AI in law is ethical, not merely technical. It requires confronting the essential qualities of judgment. Not all decisions can, or should, be reduced to prediction. Not all fairness can be encoded.

Certain dimensions of human adjudication—empathy, responsibility, interpretive flexibility, moral accountability—resist quantification. Recognising what is lost when these faculties are minimised or outsourced is the first step toward preserving them.

Remaining human in the loop is more than a procedural afterthought; it is an act of attentiveness. It requires seeing the person, the stakes, and the power asymmetries embedded in each decision. It demands fidelity to procedural justice, even when expediency tempts us toward automation. The critical question becomes not whether a model is accurate, but whether it is just. Meeting that standard calls for a specific literacy—not only data fluency, but institutional consciousness: a nuanced understanding of how legal systems operate, where discretion resides, and why certain elements of justice must resist optimisation.

This literacy extends beyond legal professionals. In an age where authority is encoded in algorithms, civic understanding becomes a public necessity. Predictive tools now influence realms from child welfare to immigration; citizens must be equipped to interrogate, contest, and contextualise these systems. Otherwise, the gap between governed and governors deepens into an abyss of passive deference. The questions "Who built this system? What assumptions were encoded? Which alternatives were excluded?" are no longer optional—they are essential to civic engagement.

Acquiring this literacy entails discomfort. The disillusionment that follows a thorough audit of legal AI is not failure; it is awakening. It is the recognition that "smart courts" are a misnomer if transparency is absent, that fairness metrics are hollow without community input, and that trust in AI is meaningless if it demands unquestioning compliance. Knowing what is wrong sharpens our sense of what must be defended.

Defence begins by naming what matters. This chapter invites readers to articulate their irreducibles—the domains, principles, or human capacities that must remain sovereign in a digitised legal order. For some, this may be the right to a human judge; for others, the preservation of community-based justice practices, immune to algorithmic scaling. Whatever the boundary, naming it is essential.

Without such definition, less accountable actors will decide where human judgment ends and machine logic begins.

Drawing the line is not enough; it must be actively held. This entails embedding contestability throughout legal AI systems: procedural mechanisms allowing challenges to automated outcomes, demands for explanation, and invocation of alternative paths. It means educating future lawyers to interrogate AI critically, ethically, and historically. It means building institutions that are not merely digitised, but democratised.

Finally, understanding these systems is not a professional luxury; it is a civic responsibility. When power increasingly flows through algorithms, when discretion is coded rather than legislated, ignorance equates to voicelessness. The antidote is literacy, vigilance, and engagement.

This chapter closes not with neat resolution, but with reorientation. Knowledge of AI's impact on law is also an opportunity for clarity: to shape trajectories rather than passively accept them, to recognise risk in order to resist it, and to identify what must remain human in the administration of justice. Ultimately, the question is not what AI can do in law, but what we are prepared to allow—and, above all, what we are determined to preserve.

What We Cannot Unsee

There is a particular kind of disillusionment that arises not from scandal or failure, but from understanding. It emerges when one peers beneath the surface of institutions long trusted to arbitrate fairness—courts, asylum boards, family tribunals—and recognises their fragility. Not simply their human fallibility, which is well known, but their structural vulnerability to technologies designed without moral nuance, democratic memory, or constitutional constraint. The most unsettling truths about legal AI are not that it occasionally gets things wrong, but that it can appear procedurally sound while missing the point of justice entirely. *Once we have seen how power can be encoded, how bias can be laundered through data, and how accountability can vanish behind layers of technical abstraction, we cannot unsee it.*

The discomfort that follows is not a failure of critical reasoning—it is its awakening. For professionals steeped in legal traditions, and citizens raised to view law as a stabilising pillar of liberal democracy, the prospect of replacing interpretive judgment with predictive scoring can feel like a betrayal. That betrayal is not just theoretical. In 2016, ProPublica revealed that COMPAS, a proprietary algorithm used in several U.S. states to inform bail and sentencing decisions, disproportionately labelled Black defendants as high-risk—yet the vendor refused to disclose the model's inner workings. A tool that purported to improve objectivity ended up cloaking racial bias in statistical authority, with no way for defendants to contest its rationale. The judicial robe had been swapped for a black box.

Such cases puncture the myth that technology brings neutrality. Legal reasoning, by its very nature, is contextual, value-laden, and dialectical. It asks not simply what *is* but what *ought to be.* When machine judgment encroaches on this terrain, it often bypasses the moral texture that underpins law's legitimacy. The resulting gap is not only ethical but epistemic—what counts as valid knowledge, evidence, or inference is quietly redefined by the logic of computation. *This is not the future arriving prematurely. It is authority being reconfigured, silently.*

For those within the legal profession, this realisation can induce a quiet crisis. Law is, after all, a discipline of justification. Judges must give reasons. Advocates must persuade. Legislators must codify intentions. Yet AI systems often operate on inference chains invisible even to their designers, trained on datasets whose composition and origin remain undisclosed. How, then, does one argue with a verdict shaped by correlations no human ever reviewed? The judicial process becomes performative if its outcomes are shaped elsewhere, in codebases few understand and fewer still can interrogate. This inversion of legal architecture—where explanation follows outcome rather than precedes it—upends centuries of procedural justice.

Even the well-meaning embrace of AI in law can inadvertently deepen these dilemmas. Consider child welfare screening systems, such as those trialled in Allegheny County, Pennsylvania, which use predictive risk models to guide social workers on whom to investigate. While intended to optimise limited resources, these systems rely on historical data that reflects entrenched surveillance of poor and minority communities. The result? The system flags more children for intervention in already over-policed families, reinforcing structural disadvantage under the guise of efficiency. The tool doesn't ask whether the data reflects injustice—it operationalises it. *Technological fluency without ethical literacy is not progress. It is acceleration in the wrong direction.*

And yet, disillusionment is not paralysis. It is the precondition for deeper moral clarity. The fact that legal AI systems reveal law's pre-existing biases does not absolve those who build or deploy them. On the contrary, it sharpens the imperative to name where lines must be drawn. Not all disillusionment is destructive. Sometimes, it clears the ground for better questions. What are the boundaries of delegation? What human faculties—empathy, moral imagination, interpretive subtlety—are non-negotiable in adjudication? What systemic protections must be designed *before* AI systems are introduced, not as afterthoughts?

Some technologists argue that greater transparency is the answer. If we can explain what the algorithm is doing, they suggest, legitimacy follows. But explanation is not a substitute for judgment. A decision can be entirely explainable and still deeply unjust. What's missing is not just clarity, but *contestability*. The ability to interrogate, resist, and revise decisions is what makes legal authority legitimate—not the cleanliness of the code that generated them. Here, the danger lies in a subtle shift: from law as a forum for contest to law as a function of prediction.

This shift is not hypothetical. It is already taking root in the bureaucracies of migration, taxation, and benefit allocation. In the Netherlands, the SyRI (System Risk Indication) programme cross-referenced citizens' data to flag fraud risk in welfare claims—effectively creating a social credit system without public debate. Courts later ruled it violated privacy and non-discrimination rights.

But for years, it operated unchecked. The system's opacity was not a bug—it was its design. It ensured efficiency by making accountability hard to locate.

For the conscientious reader, such examples can erode confidence not only in technology, but in the institutions that embraced it. If governments deploy opaque algorithms to decide who gets housing, safety, or liberty—often without notice, explanation, or recourse—what does that say about the health of democratic oversight? The tension is not merely procedural. It is constitutional. AI in law is not just a tool. It is a force that redistributes power—often upward, away from those most affected by its decisions. *To see this clearly is to accept that the threats AI poses to law are not speculative—they are structural.*

Still, the aim is not to induce cynicism, but moral resolve. Disillusionment is uncomfortable because it ruptures our sense of institutional innocence. But innocence is not the same as virtue. Institutions, like individuals, are capable of growth only when they are stripped of illusions. To see clearly is to be positioned to act ethically. It means designing systems where dissent is possible, where discretion is traceable, and where the people affected retain voice and visibility. It means resisting the seduction of optimisation when what's needed is deliberation. It means remembering that speed is not justice, and prediction is not judgment.

The work ahead, then, is not only technical. It is civic, pedagogical, and moral. Law schools must teach not just statutes and precedents, but data ethics, system design, and the politics of classification. Civil society must demand legal technologies that serve public values, not private efficiencies. Technologists must embed democratic safeguards into architecture, not layer them on after deployment. Citizens must learn to ask better questions: *Who owns this system? Who benefits from its errors? Who decides what it optimises for?*

We cannot unsee what has been revealed by the rise of legal AI. But neither should we wish to. That clarity is a resource—perhaps the most vital one we possess. It allows us to navigate complexity without retreating into naïveté or fatalism. It enables us to approach legal innovation not as a march of progress, but as a field of contested choices. It reminds us that justice is not the byproduct of efficiency, but the outcome of care, accountability, and shared moral labour. The path forward begins with that recognition—not as a burden, but as a responsibility.

Staying Human in the Loop

It is easy to mistake efficiency for virtue when digital systems promise speed, consistency, and scalability. In the legal domain, where slow processes often breed frustration and inequity, the seduction of mechanisation is especially strong. But the quest for optimisation can obscure a far deeper cost: *the erosion of human judgement as a moral anchor*. The problem is not that AI systems are becoming more capable, but that we are becoming less attentive to the question of what capabilities should remain *irrevocably human*. Staying human in the loop is not a procedural safeguard; it is a civic and ethical imperative.

Legal systems are not machines, even if they sometimes behave like ones. They are dynamic, historically situated institutions designed not merely to enforce norms, but to interrogate them—to weigh context, to accommodate dissent, to make room for mercy. Their legitimacy depends not only on consistency of output but on the *manner of reasoning* and the *moral intelligibility* of their outcomes. Automation risks transforming legal judgment into legal computation, flattening the deeply human dimensions of dispute—ambiguity, empathy, remorse—into pattern recognition and optimisation goals.

This is not an abstract concern. Across jurisdictions, AI tools are already shaping decisions in areas as sensitive as bail, parole, child custody, welfare eligibility, and asylum determination. These tools are often described as "assistive," but their influence is rarely neutral. When judges are presented with algorithmic scores or predictions, those outputs acquire epistemic weight. They suggest objectivity. They carry the sheen of data-driven impartiality. And yet the datasets on which they are trained often encode the historical biases they purport to transcend. Human discretion may remain technically present, but it is psychologically and institutionally subordinated. The human becomes a rubber stamp.

Resisting this drift requires more than slowing the adoption of legal AI. It requires a conscious and continuous reaffirmation of the *stakes* that define human judgment—what is at risk, what cannot be programmed, what must be deliberated. Institutions must be reoriented not around what machines can do, but around what only humans should. This means foregrounding questions of narrative, dignity, and conscience—elements that evade algorithmic capture yet are central to just outcomes.

One of the most vital contexts for this conversation is child welfare proceedings. In the United States, predictive analytics tools have been deployed in jurisdictions like Allegheny County to assess the likelihood of child maltreatment based on family data. While these systems aim to allocate social work resources more efficiently, they can deepen racial and socioeconomic inequities by over-surveilling already-marginalised communities. A single mother receiving public assistance might be flagged as "high-risk" based on proxies—poverty, neighbourhood, past contact with social services—rather than actual harm. Once flagged, her interactions with the system may become self-fulfilling: more scrutiny, more interventions, more presumed risk. Here, the algorithm doesn't simply assist human judgment; it distorts and disciplines it.

In such contexts, the human in the loop must not be a passive checkpoint. *They must be empowered to question, to override, to resist.* That requires cultivating cultures of deliberation, not compliance. Professionals must be trained not only in how to use AI tools but in when and why to refuse their guidance. This calls for *institutional redesign*—spaces for reflection, dissent mechanisms, accountability structures that treat human judgment as a site of responsibility rather than liability.

Equally important is the role of *civic literacy*. Citizens interacting with legal systems—whether as plaintiffs, defendants, or petitioners—must understand how decisions affecting them are made. If algorithms are involved, they must be visible, contestable, and explicable in human terms. It is not enough to disclose that a tool was used; people must have the right to ask *why*, to challenge its reasoning, to demand review by a human who listens, not a system that scores. This right of contestation is not a technical feature but a democratic necessity.

The deeper challenge lies in resisting the narrative that algorithmic recommendations are epistemically superior because they are statistically derived. Human judgment is fallible, yes—but it is *accountably* fallible. Its weaknesses can be interrogated in the open, subjected to appeal, reshaped by empathy or remorse. An AI system that fails may do so invisibly, insidiously, and at scale. It cannot be cross-examined. It does not regret.

Some jurisdictions have begun to push back. In the Netherlands, the SyRI (System Risk Indication) tool—a state-run AI system that analysed data to detect welfare fraud—was struck down by the courts in 2020 for violating privacy and transparency rights. The ruling was more than a data protection victory; it was an affirmation that automated suspicion must not replace public reason. In France, the Conseil d'État has imposed limits on the use of predictive tools in judicial contexts, arguing that algorithmic guidance must not override judicial independence. These developments offer a counter-model: one where the *preservation of human judgment is treated as a constitutional value*, not a legacy constraint.

But the most powerful acts of resistance may occur at the micro level—when a judge refuses to defer to an opaque risk score, when a caseworker overrides an algorithmic flag, when a defendant challenges an automated recommendation and insists on being heard. These moments are small but significant. They reclaim *agency*. They reassert that the law is not a service, but a moral enterprise.

None of this is to suggest a wholesale rejection of technology. Used well, AI can assist in reducing delays, uncovering patterns of discrimination, or identifying inconsistent rulings across jurisdictions. But these gains must not come at the cost of *flattening the moral topography* of legal reasoning. Efficiency is not synonymous with justice. Prediction is not understanding. Precision is not wisdom.

Staying human in the loop means making space for hesitation, for ambivalence, for the slow work of ethical discernment. It means building systems that amplify—not sideline—the irreplaceable capacities of human conscience. This includes the capacity to see nuance, to change one's mind, to weep over a decision. No algorithm, however sophisticated, can be accountable in the way a person can be—because only persons can *care*.

The future of legal AI will not be shaped solely by technical innovation or legislative fiat. It will be shaped by the habits of those who operate within the system: their courage to pause, their insistence on listening, their refusal to cede their judgment to machinery. That is the heart of the human loop—not presence, but *participation*. Not compliance, but conscience.

To defend human judgment is not to romanticise it. It is to defend the conditions under which accountability, empathy, and dissent remain possible. And in doing so, it is to defend democracy itself.

Naming What Matters

Not everything that can be automated should be. That distinction—between technical feasibility and moral permissibility—is fast becoming one of the most urgent questions of our time. As artificial intelligence extends its reach into legal reasoning, governance, medicine, education, and war, the stakes of that distinction are no longer speculative. They are personal, institutional, and civilisational. It is no longer sufficient to ask what machines *can* do; we must decide, with clarity and conviction, what they *must not*. This is not a conversation for engineers alone, nor for legal theorists in isolation. It is a civic duty, a democratic reckoning. *Naming what matters* is the act of drawing lines in the sand—not in defiance of progress, but in defence of principle.

This act requires more than caution; it requires discernment. The ethical terrain of automation is not a binary map of red and green zones. It is a topography of ambiguity, where many decisions involve trade-offs among efficiency, fairness, human dignity, and public trust. And yet some domains demand bright lines—non-negotiable boundaries beyond which automation should not go, regardless of how "safe" or "accurate" it appears. These boundaries must be drawn not only in code, but in culture: in our institutional norms, our public values, and our shared sense of what it means to treat each other as moral agents rather than datapoints.

Consider the question of moral culpability. Criminal sentencing, for instance, is not merely a question of actuarial risk. It is a societal judgment about responsibility, accountability, and justice. And while AI systems can be trained to predict recidivism rates, their predictions cannot capture remorse, rehabilitation, or the unique narrative of a defendant's life. To outsource such decisions to an algorithm—even one couched in "transparency" or explainability—is to flatten the moral texture of justice into numerical correlation. It erodes the communicative function of the law: that those subject to its power deserve to be judged as individuals, not as averages. *This is a line worth drawing.*

Or take end-of-life care. Clinical algorithms can suggest treatment plans, but they cannot grasp the existential weight of dying, the sacredness of last words, the unique obligations borne by a physician who must look a family in the eye. To allow AI to triage human lives based solely on resource allocation models—however efficient—is to sever decision-making from compassion. In such moments, humanity is not a flaw in the system; it is the point of the system. *This too is a line worth defending.*

But drawing lines is only the beginning. We must also be willing to *name* what is at stake. Language matters. Sanitised terms like "optimisation," "efficiency," or "decision-support" can obscure the ethical reality of what is being surrendered. When a welfare recipient is denied benefits by an opaque scoring system, that is not "data-driven administration." It is *the withdrawal of moral accountability.* When an asylum seeker is rejected based on a pattern-matching algorithm trained on past approvals, it is not "streamlining." It is *the automation of exclusion.* Naming what matters means refusing the euphemisms of technocracy. It means restoring the moral vocabulary necessary to debate what justice demands.

This act of naming also requires *institutional courage.* Legislators, judges, educators, and civil servants must articulate where automation ends—and why. This is especially difficult in political cultures obsessed with efficiency and fearful of appearing anti-innovation. But the preservation of human judgment cannot be left to inertia. It must be codified in law, taught in professional training, embedded in public expectations. This means, for instance, passing legislation that guarantees the right to human review in high-stakes decisions. It means establishing oversight bodies that include ethicists, affected communities, and not just data scientists. It means designing systems that invite—not resist—human challenge.

Some countries have begun to recognise this. The European Union's AI Act, for example, categorises certain uses of AI in the public sector as "high-risk" and requires safeguards such as human oversight and the right to explanation. But even these efforts risk treating human review as a procedural afterthought rather than a normative commitment. What is needed is not just better compliance mechanisms, but a cultural shift: one that recognises *judgment as a form of care*, not merely a checkpoint.

At the personal level, naming what matters calls for moral clarity about what one is willing to do—or not do—in the name of automation. For professionals in law, medicine, education, and public service, this may mean resisting pressures to defer to algorithmic systems, even at institutional cost. It may mean whistleblowing. It may mean slowing down processes that technology could accelerate, because speed would erode dignity. These are not easy stances to take. But they are necessary if we are to prevent human responsibility from being displaced by technical delegation.

Importantly, this is not a rejection of AI, nor a call for Luddite resistance. Well-designed AI systems can augment human decision-making, flag bias, increase consistency, and process information at scales that no person could manage alone. The question is not whether to use AI, but *how, where, and under whose terms*. A surgeon may use robotic assistance for precision, but the decision to operate—and how to explain its risks—must remain hers. A judge may use tools to assess sentencing disparities, but not to abdicate her own deliberation. A social worker may use data to identify families in need, but not to override her face-to-face understanding of a child's context.

The litmus test is simple but demanding: does the use of AI *diminish* the human capacity for responsibility, empathy, and judgment? If it does, then it must be resisted. If it enhances those capacities without erasing them, it may be welcomed—with caution, accountability, and humility.

This principle must be taught. In law schools, ethics seminars, corporate boardrooms, and public service training. We must teach not only how to *use* AI, but how to *refuse* it—when refusal is necessary. We must equip professionals to articulate their lines, to defend them, and to see such defence not as inefficiency but as *integrity*. Only then can democratic societies retain the moral infrastructure required to govern wisely in the age of intelligent machines.

What we choose to leave human says as much about our values as what we choose to automate. To leave space for human judgment is to affirm that some decisions carry *moral weight*—weight that cannot be computed, only borne. That some interactions are not problems to be solved but relationships to be navigated. That some forms of care, justice, and dignity are meaningful precisely because they are fallible, slow, and accountable.

Naming what matters is not a luxury. It is the first line of defence against a world where decisions are made *about* people, without being made *with* them. It is a practice of remembering that the legitimacy of our institutions rests not on their predictive accuracy, but on their moral credibility. And it is a call—to lawyers, judges, technologists, educators, and citizens alike—to take a stance not just on what is possible, but on what is *right*.

Clarity as Civic Power

Understanding how a system works is no longer a luxury reserved for technical specialists. In a society increasingly governed by code—where algorithmic outputs determine mortgage approvals, parole outcomes, tax audits, and even battlefield targeting—grasping the logic behind digital decision-making is a form of *civic literacy*. And like all forms of civic literacy, it is a precondition for meaningful participation, informed dissent, and legitimate governance. The future of democracy may hinge not just on access to information, but on the *clarity* with which that information is understood, questioned, and used to hold power accountable.

This is not a rhetorical flourish. Around the world, governments and private institutions are delegating consequential choices to automated systems. In theory, such systems promise efficiency, consistency, and objectivity. In practice, they often operate as black boxes—complex, data-driven engines whose inner workings are inaccessible not only to the public, but often to those charged with overseeing them. When authority becomes opaque, and citizens lack the tools to interrogate its logic, we move from a rule of law to a rule of signals. We risk replacing consent with compliance, and legitimacy with inertia.

The core problem is not the presence of technology, but the absence of legibility. An AI system used to detect benefits fraud might be technically impressive, statistically accurate, and legally sanctioned—but if its operation cannot be explained to those it affects, or meaningfully challenged by those who suspect error, then it operates outside the bounds of democratic accountability. Clarity, in this context, is not a technical feature. It is a political demand. And meeting it requires more than better interfaces or simplified dashboards. It demands an investment in public understanding—of algorithms, of law, and of the places where they now overlap.

Consider the Dutch childcare benefits scandal, in which thousands of families were wrongfully accused of fraud by an algorithmic system that flagged them for minor or bureaucratic inconsistencies. The system was opaque, and those accused had little recourse to understand or challenge the judgments made. Many were financially ruined. Trust in public institutions eroded, not just because mistakes were made, but because *no one could explain how* or *why* the decisions had been reached. This was not a technical failure. It was a democratic one. The lesson is clear: opacity is not a neutral state. It creates asymmetries of power, insulating decision-makers from scrutiny and disempowering those affected.

The antidote is not simply transparency in the narrow sense. Posting code repositories or disclosing datasets is insufficient if the people most impacted cannot parse them. What's needed is *contextual intelligibility*—the ability for laypersons to understand, at the point of impact, how a decision was made, what data it relied on, what assumptions it embedded, and how it can be contested. This requires both system design and civic education. Without the former, even well-informed citizens will hit walls of technical obfuscation. Without the latter, even the most interpretable systems will be misread or misused.

Civic power, in the age of encoded authority, depends on cultivating this clarity at multiple levels. For technologists, it means designing systems that *anticipate interrogation*—systems that come with built-in mechanisms for justification, audit, and counter-argument. For policymakers, it means embedding standards of interpretability, challengeability, and human review into procurement contracts and regulatory frameworks. For journalists, educators, and civil society actors, it means translating complex technical phenomena into narratives that resonate without distorting. And for ordinary citizens, it means embracing a new dimension of civic duty: learning not just how to vote or protest, but how to read the outputs of the systems that increasingly shape public life.

This clarity is not just defensive. It is empowering. Understanding how a sentencing algorithm works enables a defence lawyer to challenge its use in court. Grasping the assumptions behind a predictive policing tool allows a community to demand evidence-based limits. Knowing how a public benefits algorithm scores eligibility can help claimants advocate for fairer rules. In each case, clarity transforms from a passive awareness into an *active lever of agency*.

But clarity also has limits—and these too must be acknowledged with intellectual honesty. Not all systems can be fully understood by all people at all times. Some models are too complex, their data pipelines too vast, their statistical logic too foreign to human intuition. In such cases, the goal should not be to make every citizen an AI expert. Rather, it should be to establish *institutional intermediaries of trust*: regulatory bodies, public interest technologists, legal advocates, and independent auditors who are tasked with making sense of the system on the public's behalf, and who are held to account for that role.

This, in turn, raises a deeper question: who gets to define what clarity means? In some cases, governments have used the language of clarity to enforce superficial compliance—tick-box explainability requirements that do little to illuminate actual function. In others, corporations have deployed selectively "interpretable" models that conceal underlying biases or trade secrets. If clarity is to function as civic power rather than institutional window dressing, it must be defined from the perspective of those most affected—not just those who build or regulate the systems.

There is a precedent for this in law. Legal systems have long recognised the principle that rules must be *knowable*, that judgments must be *reasoned*, and that power must be *appealable*. These are not just procedural niceties—they are the scaffolding of legitimacy. As algorithmic systems take on quasi-legal functions, those same principles must be reasserted in digital form. It is not enough for an AI system to comply with privacy or anti-discrimination statutes. It must be designed to allow those subjected to its decisions to *understand, question, and correct them.*

This is particularly crucial in contexts of structural inequality. When marginalised communities are subject to algorithmic surveillance, automated welfare assessments, or predictive risk scores, the absence of clarity compounds existing injustices. To demand clarity is, therefore, not a mere procedural ask—it is a demand for *epistemic justice*, the right to be intelligible to the systems that govern one's life, and the right to contest misrepresentation.

None of this will happen on its own. The incentives of markets, institutions, and even professional cultures often run counter to clarity. Complexity creates barriers to entry. Obfuscation protects against liability. Proprietary models promise competitive advantage. The burden of making systems intelligible is rarely rewarded, and the cost of ignorance is often borne by those least able to absorb it. It is therefore up to the civic sphere—educators, watchdogs, professional associations, public interest technologists—to elevate clarity from a design preference to a *normative expectation.*

Doing so will require investment: in education, in public infrastructure, in cross-disciplinary collaboration. But it will also require imagination—a willingness to treat clarity not as a constraint, but as a design principle that shapes how we build, deploy, and govern technology. When systems are clear, they can be corrected. When they are legible, they can be negotiated. When they are accountable, they can be trusted. This is the foundation not just of better technology, but of a more democratic society.

Understanding how encoded systems function—and insisting on their legibility—is no longer the domain of specialists alone. It is the responsibility of all who live under their influence. In this sense, clarity is not just a technical virtue or a policy goal. It is *civic power*: the capacity to see, to question, and to act. And in the face of automated authority, it may be the most important form of power we have left.

About the Author

Corin Hale writes about the ethical limits of technology, the fragility of systems, and the tensions between speed, scale, and justice. With a background steeped in institutional research and a deep skepticism of techno-solutionism, Hale brings a clear-eyed voice to the most pressing questions facing the legal world in the age of automation. His work examines how AI doesn't just change tools—it reshapes authority, accountability, and what we understand as judgment itself. Judgment by Code is his defining exploration of what we risk when we let machines take the bench.

www.ingramcontent.com/pod-product-compliance
Lightning Source LLC
Chambersburg PA
CBHW031345230926
51848CB00002B/388